First World War
and Army of Occupation
War Diary
France, Belgium and Germany

40 DIVISION
Divisional Troops
178 Brigade Royal Field Artillery
2 June 1916 - 31 March 1919

WO95/2598/1

The Naval & Military Press Ltd
www.nmarchive.com
Published in association with The National Archives

Published by

The Naval & Military Press Ltd

Unit 10 Ridgewood Industrial Park,
Uckfield, East Sussex,
TN22 5QE England
Tel: +44 (0) 1825 749494

www.naval-military-press.com
www.nmarchive.com

This diary has been reprinted in facsimile from the original. Any imperfections are inevitably reproduced and the quality may fall short of modern type and cartographic standards.

© **Crown Copyright**
Images reproduced by permission of The National Archives, London, England, 2015.

Contents

Document type	Place/Title	Date From	Date To
Heading	WO95/2598/1 178 Brigade Royal Field Ambulance		
Heading	178th Brigade R.F.A. Jun 1916-Mar 1919		
Miscellaneous	C Form (Duplicate). Messages And Signals.		
War Diary	Deepcut	02/06/1916	02/06/1916
War Diary	Farnborough	02/06/1916	02/06/1916
War Diary	Southampton	02/06/1916	02/06/1916
War Diary	Havre	03/06/1916	04/06/1916
War Diary	Berguette	05/06/1916	05/06/1916
War Diary	Bellary	06/06/1916	13/06/1916
War Diary	Loos Salient	14/06/1916	07/07/1916
War Diary	Les Brebis	08/07/1916	23/09/1916
War Diary	Mazingarbe	24/09/1916	11/10/1916
War Diary	Philosophe	12/10/1916	31/10/1916
Miscellaneous	Left Group Operation Order	02/10/1916	02/10/1916
Miscellaneous	Left Group Order No. 5	20/10/1916	20/10/1916
Miscellaneous	Table A		
Miscellaneous	Strafe-Ing	31/10/1916	31/10/1916
War Diary	Philosophe	01/11/1916	30/11/1916
Miscellaneous	Minor Operation	12/11/1916	12/11/1916
Miscellaneous			
Miscellaneous	To O.C. D/178th Bde. R.F.A.	14/11/1916	14/11/1916
Miscellaneous	O.C. B/178	14/11/1918	14/11/1918
War Diary	Philosophe	01/12/1916	04/12/1916
War Diary	Lapugnoy	05/12/1916	05/12/1916
War Diary	Ostreville	06/12/1916	06/12/1916
War Diary	Vacquerie	07/12/1916	07/12/1916
War Diary	Amplier	08/12/1916	08/12/1916
War Diary	Villers Bocage	09/12/1916	09/12/1916
War Diary	Camp 14 Near-Bray	10/12/1916	10/12/1916
War Diary	Camp 14 Bray	11/12/1916	13/12/1916
War Diary	Near Comble Arderlu Wood	14/12/1916	19/12/1916
War Diary	Bois Du Anderlu Nr Combles	20/12/1916	28/12/1916
War Diary	Anderlu Wood Nr Combles	29/12/1916	31/12/1916
War Diary		01/01/1917	30/06/1917
War Diary	In The Field	01/07/1917	31/10/1917
Miscellaneous	Centre Group	26/10/1917	26/10/1917
War Diary	In The Field	01/11/1917	31/01/1918
War Diary	Field	01/02/1918	28/02/1918
Miscellaneous	Right Group	09/02/1918	09/02/1918
Miscellaneous	Right Group	15/02/1918	15/02/1918
Miscellaneous	Right Group	20/02/1918	20/02/1918
Miscellaneous	54th Bde. R.G.A.	24/02/1918	24/02/1918
Miscellaneous	Left Group 59th D.A.	21/02/1918	21/02/1918
Miscellaneous	Left Group 59th D.A.	22/02/1918	22/02/1918
Miscellaneous	Left Group 59th D.A.	23/02/1918	23/02/1918
Miscellaneous	Left Group 59th D.A.	24/02/1918	24/02/1918
Miscellaneous	Left Group 59th D.A.	25/02/1918	25/02/1918
Miscellaneous	Left Group 59th D.A.	26/02/1918	26/02/1918
Heading	178th Brigade. Royal Field Artillery March 1918		
War Diary	In The Field	01/03/1918	22/03/1918

War Diary	Field	23/03/1918	28/03/1918
War Diary	In The Field	29/03/1918	31/03/1918
Heading	178th Brigade Royal Field Artillery April 1918		
War Diary	Field	01/04/1918	25/04/1918
War Diary	In The Field	26/05/1918	06/06/1918
War Diary	Field	07/06/1918	11/07/1918
War Diary	In The Field	12/07/1918	26/07/1918
War Diary	Field	27/07/1918	31/07/1918
War Diary	In The Field	01/08/1918	31/10/1918
War Diary	Field	01/11/1918	21/01/1919
War Diary	France	21/01/1919	21/01/1919
War Diary	Marquette	01/02/1919	28/02/1919
War Diary	Wainbrechies	01/03/1919	31/03/1919

WO95/2598/1

178 Brigade Royal Field Artillery

40TH DIVISION

178TH BRIGADE R.F.A.
JUN 1916 - MAR 1919.

2598

"C" Form (Duplicate).
MESSAGES AND SIGNALS.
Army Form C. 2123.
No. of Message

AB 65 Dco
SB

Service Instructions.

Handed in at .... Front .... Office 1.10 p.m. Received 1.20 p.m.

TO 4↑ Divn

Sender's Number	Day of Month	In reply to Number	AAA
G 343	29th	Mar.	

The two batteries of the 47th Divn which are being pulled out tonight should remain in the 2nd Divn area as a reserve to the 2nd Divl artillery aaa 2nd Division will arrange for the accommodation of these batteries aaa added 47th Divn rptd 47 Divn arty 2nd Divn RA & Corps and G.4 Corps

FROM Fourth Corps
PLACE & TIME 1.10 pm

WAR DIARY
or
INTELLIGENCE SUMMARY
(Erase heading not required.)

Army Form C. 2118

June 1 1916

198th Bde R.F.A. Vol 1

Commanded by Lt. Col. D.H. Gill R.F.A.

Place	Date	Hour	Summary of Events and Information	Remarks and references to Appendices
DEEPCUT	2·6·16	6.30	First portion of 178th Bde R.F.A. left DEEPCUT for FARNBOROUGH	
FARNBOROUGH	—	11.30	Brigade entrained by to Railway at intervals of ½ hr for SOUTHAMPTON	
—	—	8.15	Brigade entrained in two portions for HARVE	
SOUTHAMPTON	—	16.00	Brigade commenced to disembark & as soon as ready proceeded to 90's Rest Camp remaining	
HARVE	3·6·16	9.0	there one night	
—	4·6·16	8.0	Brigade commenced to entrain by batteries at intervals of 5 hrs & proceeded to BERGUETTE via ROUEN - ABBEVILLE & LILLERS, the journey taking about 20 hours	
BERGUETTE	5·6·16	3.0	Batteries detrained & proceeded direct to Billeting Area in vicinity of BELLARY, last Battery arriving at billets about 16.00 o'ck.	
BELLARY	6·6·16		Days devoted to cleaning up & adjusting minor casualties to equipment etc.	
—	7·6·16			
—	8·6·16		Brigade & Battery commanders provided by Motor Bus to NOEUX-LES-MINES to view positions occupied by Training Battalion. Ref sheet 36 B K.18 d., returning the same day	
—	9·6·16		Bde HQ & left administration staff, & sections of A.B.C &D Batteries proceeded by March Route to front line for attachment & training to the following units. A Battery to 110th Bde., HQ & B to 125th, C to 16th Bgde., D to M.A. Reserve 1st Corps.	
—	10·6·16		Remaining section of A Battery proceeded to join section with 110th Bde.	
—	11·6·16		Church Parade conducted by Capt. L.E.O Bawden R.F.A.	
—	12·6·16		Orders received & remainder of Brigade prepared to proceed to firing line	
—	13·6·16		Section march at 20 min intervals proceeding via LILLERS - BETHUNE - SAILLY-LA-BOURSE	

WAR DIARY or INTELLIGENCE SUMMARY

Army Form C. 2118

Place	Date	Hour	Summary of Events and Information	Remarks and references to Appendices
LOOS SALIENT	14.6.16		Sections were into position on night of 13-14th as follows:- H.Q attacked to 26th Bde 1st Div. L. 56.c.1.1. A Battery CORONS-DU-RUTOIRE R Sec. G.14.d.2.2. L Sec. G.14.c.6.2. B Battery Quality Street G.27.C.8.8. C Battery M.1.6.4.2. D Battery G.14.c.9.7. Quiet day. Detachments work on Gun Pits. Registrations checked.	
	15.6.16		Very quiet day. Enemy Anti-aircraft active	
	16.6.16		Day quiet on the whole. Men employed to improve Wagon lines	
	17.6.16		Cloudy day. Occasional shelling on our front + Support line trenches with light guns.	
	18.6.16		Again cloudy. Reg explosion heard in COLONNE at 11-0 am.	
	19.6.16		Clear morning. Aeroplane activity.	
	20.6.16		Dull morning. Trench Mortars active. Enemy reply with some H.E. 2 on our front + support line	
	21.6.16		Very fine day. 10 balloons up. Much aeroplane activity	
	22.6.16		Clear day. Aircraft again active. Occasional shelling by both sides, + Trench mortar activity near HART'S CRATER.	

WAR DIARY
or
INTELLIGENCE SUMMARY
(Erase heading not required.)

Army Form C. 2118

Instructions regarding War Diaries and Intelligence Summaries are contained in F. S. Regs., Part II. and the Staff Manual respectively. Title Pages will be prepared in manuscript.

Place	Date	Hour	Summary of Events and Information	Remarks and references to Appendices
	24.6.16		Fine morning. Enemy light gun again active on our trenches. Our 18 prs retaliated.	17 N.C.O + men posted to Y. & Z. T.M. Battery
	25.6.16		Enemy again shell our trenches in the TRIANGLE. In the evening enemy bombarded with 77 m.m. 4.10.5 m.m. on communication & support trenches.	Lieut. 7/17 Gill
	26.6.16		Artillery activity on both sides during the morning. During night 25-26th our infantry raided enemy trenches in COLONNE sector. No prisoners taken by us. 12 of Raiding Party missing.	
	27.6.16	12.15 am	Heavy bombardment by our artillery & T.M's. Enemy retaliation weak.	Capt. L.E.O. Davidson carried on with duties from 23-2-16
	28.6.16		Morning quiet. Intermittent shelling by both sides during afternoon. Evening quiet.	
	29.6.16		Our 18 pr. Battery active during afternoon. Evening quiet.	
	30.6.16	9.30 pm	Morning quiet on the whole. Enemy apparently registering several points in our sector. C. Battery shelled from M.22-D flashes observed.	

40 July
Army Form C. 2118
178 RFA
Vol 2

WAR DIARY
or
INTELLIGENCE SUMMARY
(Erase heading not required.)

Place	Date	Hour	Summary of Events and Information	Remarks and references to Appendices
LOOS SALIENT	July 1st	6.30 am	Out warning. C Battery again shelled. Our gun blinds with large splinter of shell, necessitating withdrawal from action. Later part of the day quiet.	
	2nd		Quiet day except Trench Mortar activity on both sides. Orders received to relieve 1st Division.	
	3rd		Day again quiet. On night of A, B, C + 1 section E.D. move to relieve batteries of 1st Division. A Battery relieve 113th at P.5.d.3.8, C Battery L-2 relieve 114th at L.7.36.c.9t-1, C Battery relieve 117th at P.5.d.7.36.c.2-7 + D relieve H.Q. Battery R.11.b.L.7.	
	4th		See of D Battery move into new position. Lt. Col. Guise assumes command of the Right Group H.Q. D.A. composed of 178th Bde R.F.A. + B + C 185th Bde R.F.A. + 1 gun of D/185th Bde R.F.A. Battery check registrations taken over from 1st Div. Very quiet day.	
	5th		Day quiet on the whole. Intermittent shelling of our front lines with .77 from direction of LIEVIN.	
	6th			
	7th		Trench Mortar activity on M.20-c.4.4. Front trenches shelled at irregular intervals with 4.2" from LENS.	

Rutledge 2/Lt
Adjt 178 Bde RFA

WAR DIARY
or
INTELLIGENCE SUMMARY
(Erase heading not required.)

Army Form C. 2118

Place	Date	Hour	Summary of Events and Information	Remarks and references to Appendices
LES BRÉBIS	8th July 1916		Quiet day. Usual T.M. activity on both sides. Infantry report 3 or 4 5.9's near their H.Q. We retaliated.	
	9th	4.0 am	S.O.S. Signal sent up. Infantry in error? Batteries however opened fire. B. Battery being exceptionally prompt. Remainder of day Quiet.	
	10th		Quiet day. Some slight T.M. activity M.20.a.6.3.	
	11th		Quiet day. Observation excellent. F.O.O. report considerable movement on road running N.E. & S.W. just S. of St PIERRE Church M.11.c.+d.	
	12th		Slight activity on part of hostile artillery & retaliation by our guns. D/178 9 guns 3 divns joined Bde from Corps. Lieut M.H.S. Thomas posted to A/178. New B.C. order book is D/178.	
	13th		Quiet day, nothing of interest to record. 2nd/1st Staffs posted to H.Q D.A.C. Lieut A. Murray from Hotchkiss Sec to D/178. New S.J. Whilley posted to C/178 from C/188.	
	14th		The usual shelling by hostile artillery at long intervals and retaliation by our own.	

WAR DIARY or INTELLIGENCE SUMMARY

Army Form C. 2118

Place	Date	Hour	Summary of Events and Information	Remarks and references to Appendices
NOEUX LES MINES / LES BREBIS	15th		Day generally quiet. Practised aeroplane cooperation, with some success.	
	16th		Some intermittent shelling by both sides.	
	17th		A very misty day, consequently very quiet.	
	18th		On night of 18th–19th Battery carried out Species operation with Infantry. Wire was cut during day and after a heavy bombardment of the enemy trenches commencing at 12.15 am, the 18th Welsh Raiding party entered the German trenches for the purpose of obtaining information as to the forces opposing them and if possible a partial prisoner. Although their principal objective was not attained, the raid was a success, 1 Officer & 16 Rank & File & joined Brigade from Givenchy.	
	19th			
	20th	9.20 & 9.40	Day again very quiet. Slight T.M. activity only. C. Battery received attention from the Hun; their position being shelled with H.E. 2" & 5.9". Resulting in considerable damage to one gun pit, but fortunately no damage to men or equipment.	
	21st		A quiet day. Scrubber M.15.b.2–3 & Railway M.15.b.2–3 & Railway M.15.b.2.4 shelled from LIEVIN.	

Army Form C. 2118

WAR DIARY
or
INTELLIGENCE SUMMARY
(Erase heading not required.)

Instructions regarding War Diaries and Intelligence Summaries are contained in F. S. Regs., Part II. and the Staff Manual respectively. Title Pages will be prepared in manuscript.

Place	Date	Hour	Summary of Events and Information	Remarks and references to Appendices
LES BRÉBIS	22nd July 1916		Slight T.M. activity, otherwise quiet.	
	23rd		Quiet day.	
	24th		Generally speaking a quiet day. Slight shelling of support line in neighbourhood of CALONNE.	
	25th		Nothing of which to record. Slight shelling of our front line during the day by hostile artillery & retaliation by our own.	
	26th		Slightly increased activity on the part of hostile artillery.	
	27th		Considerable T.M. activity in vicinity of DOUBLE CRASSIER. Of H-30 p.m. a few rounds of H.2 fire in LES BRÉBIS. We retaliation on LIEVIN.	
	28th		Our front line and support trenches were subjected to intermittent shelling during the day. We retaliated on their front & support lines.	
	29th		The usual activity on the front of known artillery & T.M. very extensive, and no retaliation has been about normal.	

1875. Wt. W593/826 1,000,000 4/15 J.B.C. & A. A.D.S.S./Forms/C. 2118.

WAR DIARY
or
INTELLIGENCE SUMMARY
(Erase heading not required.)

Army Form C. 2118

Instructions regarding War Diaries and Intelligence Summaries are contained in F. S. Regs., Part II. and the Staff Manual respectively. Title Pages will be prepared in manuscript.

Place	Date	Hour	Summary of Events and Information	Remarks and references to Appendices
LES BREBIS	30/7/16		Enemy artillery still above normal, principally 7.7 mm. early morning very active. Shade temperature midday 79°.	
	31/7/16		Enemy light artillery & T.M.s still very active. Heavy artillery, 2nd Suys Battery called on to retaliate for T.M.s. Very hot day.	

D. Winterby E. 2/Lt.
Adjutant. 1/8th Bde R.F.A.

WAR DIARY
or
INTELLIGENCE SUMMARY

Army Form C. 2118

178th Bde. R.F.A.
Commanded by Lt. Col. D.H. Guns R.F.A.

VOL 3

Place	Date	Hour	Summary of Events and Information	Remarks and references to Appendices
LES BREBIS	1/Aug/1916		General situation on our front quite normal. Intermittent shelling with 7-7's on our front & support lines in M.15.a. No retaliation on the enemy's front & support lines.	MAP 36 c S.W. 1/10000 Edition 7A
	2/8/16		During the morning an hostile aeroplane dropped bombs in LES BREBIS causing some casualties to infantry in reserve. The enemy's artillery used very active, about 120 rounds 7-7 falling on our lines in M.15.a. during the day, this necessitating considerable retaliation on our part. Evening quiet.	
	3/8/16		Comparatively quiet day.	
	4/8/16	1.30 pm	The enemy shelled the DUMP M.20.a. with 5-9's and again at 8.30 pm with 4.2". Otherwise situation normal.	
	5/8/16		Hostile artillery again fairly active. An enemy M.G. was located near PUITS 16 in action against our aeroplanes. C/178 was able to silence it.	

WAR DIARY or INTELLIGENCE SUMMARY

Army Form C. 2118

Folio 10

178th Bde. R.F.A.
Commanded by Lt. Col. Dugüid R.F.A.

Place	Date	Hour	Summary of Events and Information	Remarks and references to Appendices
LES BREBIS	6 Aug 1916		Little of interest to record. Enemy's artillery quite normal.	Stark 7th Aug
	7/8/16	2.30 pm	The enemy shelled LES BREBIS with 4.2". We retaliated on the enemy's trenches at ROLLINCOURT.	Stark 8/8/16
	8/8/16		Intermittent shelling with 77mm on our front line trenches during day, otherwise quiet.	Stark
	9/8/16		In addition to the usual shelling with 77mm, the enemy shelled CALONNE with 5.9" & 4.2"	Stark
	10/8/16		Our front line was again subjected to recurrent shelling and trench operations with 12th S.W.B.	Stark
	11/8/16		Usual activity by enemy's artillery. One Battery engaged in "in cutting" M.15.d.2.1. Our wire showing as a front. Lieut D.L. McDonald posted to 3/1/B F.L on first appointment.	Stark 11/8/16

WAR DIARY or INTELLIGENCE SUMMARY

Army Form C. 2118

148th Inf. Bde.
Commanded by Lt. Col. D. H. Gill P.S.A.

Place	Date	Hour	Summary of Events and Information	Remarks and references to Appendices
LES BREBIS	12th August 1916	12 mid.	A fairly quiet day. All Batteries cooperated with 12th S.W.B. in minor operations. Two raiding parties entered the German trenches on either side of Sap at M.15.d.21-08. Barrage put up a barrage on the following trench junctions: A/178 M.21.a.95·80, M.21.b.02·65 & M.21.b.16·70, B/178 M.21 & M.21d.35·90, M.21b.60·00, C/178 M.15.d.36·60, M.15.d.55·20 & M.15.d.70·66, D/178 on points 16 Bis. The raiding party captured a prisoner and returned to our trenches at 12·50 am. The battalion reached fire at 12·55 am.	Ref. Map 36° SW 1 1/10,000
	13/8/16	1·20 am	O.C. 12th S.W.B. reported artillery cooperation satisfactory.	Herbert Capt.
			Unusually quiet day. No attempt at retaliation for last night's raid.	Herbert Capt a Adj.
	14/8/16		Enemy's artillery again active. Our front support line trenches in M.15 a frequently shelled with 77 mm. during the day. We retaliated freely on the enemy's support trenches in M.15.r.	Herbert Capt a Adj.
	15/8/16		Enemy's artillery directed its attention to our rearward area. About 170 shells (4·2" & 5·9") fell in LES BREBIS, completely wrecked our house & caused casualties to Infantry & Civilians. 3 rounds fell in D. Bty. position causing one casualty. BULLY GRENAY was shelled.	Herbert Capt a Adj.
	16/8/16	4·30 pm 4·45 6·0 pm		

1875 Wt. W593/826 1,000,000 4/15 J.B.C. & A. A.D.S.S./Forms/C. 2118.

WAR DIARY
INTELLIGENCE SUMMARY

Army Form C. 2118

148th Brigade R.F.A.
Commanded by Lt. Col. D. H. Gee R.F.A.

Folio
12

Place	Date	Hour	Summary of Events and Information	Remarks and references to Appendices
LES BREBIS	16th Aug. 1916		A quiet day. CALONNE was shelled between 11-30 & 11-45 a.m. and very little retaliation by our Artillery necessary.	York 17/8/16 Adj.
	17/8/16		Quiet day. Nothing of interest to record.	York 17/8/16 Adj.
	18/8/16		Enemy's artillery again quiet.	York 18/8/16 Adj.
	19/8/16	12 pm	Quiet day. Batteries registered new points. Practice gas alarm.	York 19/8/16 Adj.
	20/8/16		Enemy unusually active. Retaliation between 10.35 pm & 11-35 pm. Bombarded our front and support line in M.15.a. & M.15.b. with B & C Batteries firing on the enemy's front-line in N.15.b.	Yates 21/8/16 Adj.
	21/8/16		Hostile artillery quiet. A Battery observed enemy infantry preparing to raid by 1/4 H.L.I. Capt. R. H. Railleys cut were when infantry advanced. Bombardment was initiated.	Yates 21/8/16 Adj.
	22/8/16	10.50 pm	1/4 H.L.I carried out a raid on the enemy's trenches in CORNAILLE'S Fagot. Guns artillery cooperated by putting up a barrage on the enemy's support-line and trench junction. Raid very successful. Two prisoner captured. Cornaille-	York 23/8/16 Adj.
	23/8/16		H. Battery ceased fire 12.20 am	Greenwich 23/8/16 R.n. Adj. 173/8/16 R.S.a

WAR DIARY or INTELLIGENCE SUMMARY

Army Form C. 2118

Folio 13

178th Brigade R.F.A.
Commanded by Lt Col D H Gill R.F.A.

Place	Date	Hour	Summary of Events and Information	Remarks and references to Appendices
LES BREBIS	23/8/16		Quiet day. B. Battery engaged an hostile gun at M.15.d. H2-H2 and obtained a direct hit on emplacement.	Ref Map 36 S.W.1 1/10,000 Stark Major Adj.
	24/8/16	8.10 pm 8.25 pm	Enemy's Artillery very quiet. Batteries bombarded enemy's communication trenches + lines junctions M.21.c.7.8 & M.21.c.6.5 during relief. He was known to be carrying out reliefs 23rd Oct. Sellers posted to 6/17/16 ″ ″ Gordon 3/6 ″	Stark Major Adj.
	25/8/16	5.0 am to 5.30 am	A&C Batteries bombarded Remainder of day quiet. CORNAILLES in support of Trench Mortars	Stark Major Adj.
	26/8/16		Quiet day. Our Infantry have recently been limited with a type of trench mortar and aerial darts. It is difficult to see when they are fired from; but they fall in the trenches with great accuracy. Our artillery retaliated heavily on each occasion that the Infantry was subjected to Aerial Torpedo Bombardment.	Stark Major Adj.
	27/8/16		Enemy's artillery quiet. Batteries engaged several T.M. and M.G. emplacements with good results.	Stark Major Adj.
	28/8/16		D. Battery engaged a tense in "no man's land" M.21.a.80.85, this was reported by using a signal station at sight, + was used as an ammunition & bombing store. Battery secured a direct hit.	Stark Major Adj. Rowley Lt 178 Bde R.F.A.

1875 Wt. W593/826 1,000,000 4/15 J.B.C. & A. A.D.S.S./Forms/C. 2118.

WAR DIARY
or
INTELLIGENCE SUMMARY
(Erase heading not required.)

Army Form C. 2118

14th Cdn F.A.
Commanded by Lt. Col. D.H. Guise P.S.A

Folio 13

Place	Date	Hour	Summary of Events and Information	Remarks and references to Appendices
LES BRIEBIS	29/Aug/16		A quiet day. Nothing of interest to record.	Fyffe O/C adjt.
	30/8/16		A quiet day. Observation conditions very bad.	Fyffe adjt.
	31/8/16		Enemy still very quiet.	Fyffe adjt.
			Officers: L.B. Graham posted to C/188th	
			" L.S. Brierce " 90th See. D.A.C	
			" J.M.A. Humphrey " 69/17th	
			" Lt. Rand " "	
			" Lt. Cook " 8/178	
			" Lt. Gibson " "	
			" Lt. Baker " 5/178	
			" Lt. Biggs " 6/178	
			" Lt. Selby " 7/178	
			" Lt.L. Crookes " 4/178	

Fyffe
Adjutant 14/8/16

WAR DIARY or INTELLIGENCE SUMMARY

Army Form C. 2118

Vol 4 Folio 15

1/8th Bde R.F.A
Commanded by Lt. Col. O.H. Gee R.F.A

Place	Date	Hour	Summary of Events and Information	Remarks and references to Appendices
LES BREBIS	Sept 1st 1916		H.Q. Divisional Artillery re-organised. A.B.& C. Batteries become 6 gun Batteries. 1 Section B/185 joins A Battery, 1 Section of B/185 joins C Battery. D/185 gun ceases to command group. The CALONNE Sector is handed over to the 63rd Divisional Artillery. A Battery from new Right group H.Q. 1st D.A. & moves to position at FOSSE 7. B " " " " left " H.Q. 185 " " " " MAROC. C & D from Right group composite Arty 3rd Bde. & move to position FOSSE 7.	Stok 31/8/16 Adj
	2/9/16		2nd Lieut Y.W. Breeze B/178 posted to H.Q. D.A.E. Battens engaged in registration of new zones.	Stok 2/9/16 Adj
	3/9/16		— do —	— do — Barometer normal Temperature 65 Stok 3/9/16 Adj
	4/9/16		— do —	— do — Stok 4/9/16 Adj
	5/9/16		Enemy very quiet. Nothing of interest to record.	— do — Barometer normal Temperature 70. Stok 5/9/16 Adj
	6/9/16		Nothing to record.	— do — Stok 6/9/16 Adj

Hurbury 31/8/16
Adjutant 178 Bde R.F.A.

WAR DIARY
or
INTELLIGENCE SUMMARY
(Erase heading not required.)

Army Form C. 2118

148th Brigade R.F.A.
Comd. by Lt. Col. S.H. Gull. R.F.A.

Folio 10

Place	Date	Hour	Summary of Events and Information	Remarks and references to Appendices
LES BREBIS	Sept 7/9/16			
	8/9/16		2nd Lieut. B. Allen } posted to 39th Div. Arty. 6/7/8th	Fork rell/16 Adj.
	9/9/16			
	10/9/16		2 Lieut. W.F. Bond } posted to 41st Div. Arty. 4/7/8th H.H. Gibson 8/1/8	Nothing of Tactical Interest to record. Batteries being detached to other Groups.
	11/9/16		Lieut. H. Selby } posted to 56th Div. Arty. 8/4/8 Lieut. A. Murray	
	12/9/16			
	13/9/16			
	14/9/16			

H. Willoughby Lt H RFA Adj. 148th Bde RFA

Army Form C. 2118

WAR DIARY
or
INTELLIGENCE SUMMARY
(Erase heading not required.)

148th Brigade R.F.A.

Commanded by Lt. Col. E.H. Gwyn R.F.A.

Place	Date	Hour	Summary of Events and Information	Remarks and references to Appendices
LES BREBIS	15th Sept. 1916		C/147 & D/148 withdrew from 3rd Div. Arty. by Section. On nights of 15-16th & 16-17th Sept. and took up duty on angles of C/148 to position M.2.c.20.00 C 36.c.10.70 & D/148 to position	Map 36 c SW. 1 1/10000 Edition 7.A
	16/9/16		Lieut. Ld Elcinty'e proceeded on leave to ENGLAND. Lieut H.B. Bruyere attached to Brigade H.Q. to perform the duties of adjutant. 16th to 21st Sept. 1916	
	17/9/16		Major L.B.O. Pawden D.S.O. R.F.A. 9/148th granted leave to ENGLAND 7 days.	
	18/9/16		Lieut. Rawes posted to 3rd Divisional Artillery. Lt. Col. Gwyn conducted temporary R. Group H.Q. in relief of Lt. Col. Helmessen	
	19/9/16		Lieut. J.M.B. Honfray 8/148 posted to C/148 " " " B. Graham C/148 " " to D/148	
	20/9/16		Lt. Col. Gwyn R.F.A. relinquishes command of R. Group H.Q.	
	21/9/16		Lieut. J.U. Graham D/148 returned to H.Q. Base.	

Antony E. St. R.F.A.
Adjutant 148 Bde. R.F.A.

Army Form C. 2118

WAR DIARY
or
INTELLIGENCE SUMMARY

(Erase heading not required.)

Folio 18

148th Bde. R.F.A.

Commanded by Lt. Col. P. Gill R.F.A.

Place	Date	Hour	Summary of Events and Information	Remarks and references to Appendices
LES BREBIS	23 Sept 1916		On night of 22nd - 23rd Sept 1916 148 Brigade taken over 114 Bde Artillery Group. Lt Col Gill assumes command of 114 Bde Artillery Group to be known as Left Group 118th Bde R.F.A. Left Group 118th R.F.A. consists of A.C.D. 178 Bfys and C/161st. Remain with Centre Group 140 R.F.A. Carried out by Sections on nights of 22-23rd and 23rd-24th. Artillery reliefs carried out by Sections in vicinity of FOSSE 7. All Battery positions in vicinity of FOSSE 7.	Sgd H. P. Gill Lt Col R.F.A. Adj.
MAZENGARBE	24/9/16		Enemy's artillery very quiet. Carry out registration of new zone.	Sgd H. P. Gill Lt Col Adj.
"	25/9/16		Enemy shell our front trenches line in H 26. c. Batteries retaliate. Continue registration.	Sgd H. P. Gill Lt Col Adj.
"	26/9/16		Very quiet day. Batteries continue registration.	Sgd H. P. Gill Lt Col Adj.
"	27/9/16		Day summary quiet. Batteries still engaged in Registration.	Sgd H. P. Gill Lt Col Adj.
"	28/9/16		Quiet day.	Sgd H. P. Gill Lt Col Adj.
"	29/9/16		Left Group cooperated with 120th Inf. Brigade in minor operations on night of 29th-30th between 1.30 am & 2.0 am.	Sgd H. P. Gill Lt Col Adj.
"	30/9/16			

Lt Col H. P. Gill R.F.A.
O.C. 148 Bde R.F.A.

WAR DIARY or **INTELLIGENCE SUMMARY**
(Erase heading not required.)

Army Form C. 2118

40/VOL 5
178 Brigade R.F.A.
Commanded by Lt. Col. D.H. Gill R.F.A.

Folio 19

Place	Date	Hour	Summary of Events and Information	Remarks and references to Appendices
MAZINGARBE	1st Oct. 1916		Quiet day. No artillery activity in group sector. Barometer 30.2 Thermometer 59.	Hor 178Bde Adj.
	2/10/16		Enemy artillery again quiet. Batteries engaged 2 working parties of the enemy and retaliated for T.M. activity. Barometer 30.1 Thermometer 55. Very wet day.	Hor 178Bde Adj.
	3/10/16		Quiet day. Rain fell until midday. Barometer 30.1 Thermometer 56.	Hor 178Bde Adj.
	4/10/16		Slight activity by enemy artillery. Morning wet. Barometer normal temperature 56.	Hor 178Bde Adj.
	5/10/16		Quiet day. Very wet. Barometer 29.8. Thermometer 60. reference 6/10/16 in Left. Group.	Hor 178Bde Adj.
	6/10/16		In the night 5th–6th Left Group co-operated with 8th Division in Minor Operation. Barometer 29.9 Thermometer 60. Operation indefinitely postponed.	Hor 178Bde Adj.
	7/10/16		Quiet day. Barometer 29.9 Thermometer 61	Hor 178Bde Adj.
	8/10/16		Quiet day. Wet. Barometer normal. Thermometer 60	Hor 178Bde Adj.

Lieutenant Adjutant 178th Bde R.F.A.

WAR DIARY
INTELLIGENCE SUMMARY

Army Form C. 2118

178th Brigade R.F.A.
Commanded by Lt. Col D.H. Gill R.F.A.

Place	Date	Hour	Summary of Events and Information	Remarks and references to Appendices
MAZINGARBE	9th Oct 1916		Intermittent shelling by the enemy on our front line, otherwise quiet. Barometer 30.1 Thermometer 58.	Sgd. D.H.Gill Lt Col. R.F.A.
	10/10/16		Lt. Col D.H. Gill granted leave to England. Major S.R.O Davidson D.S.O R.F.A. assumes command of Brigade & Group. Barometer 30.1 Thermometer 59. Enemy quiet.	Sgd. S.R.O Davidson Major R.F.A.
	11/10/16		Quiet day. On night of 10-11th sections move to take up positions in HULLUCH GROUP & Lt. Div. Arty. A/178 lies two guns down in Cavite Group. Barometer 30.2 Thermometer 60. Day showery.	Sgd. S.R.O Davidson Major R.F.A.
PHILOSOPHE	12/10/16		Quiet day. Remainder of Brigade now in position as follows. A/178 G.27.c.00.20 Cavite Group. B/178 G.17.c.60.10 ? C/178 G.14.c.10.30. See A/178 G.14.9.90.90. D/178 of Group G.27.c.78.40, G.13.d.20.50 Barometer 30.2 Thermometer 56. Enemy quiet. Duel day. Balloons engaged in registration of new zones. Barometer 30.2 Thermometer 57.	Sgd. S.R.O Davidson Major R.F.A.
	13/10/16		Enemy T.Ms active in neighbourhood of HULLUCH CRATERS. Wet day. Barometer 30.1 Temperature 58.	Sgd. S.R.O Davidson Major R.F.A.
	14/10/16			

Sgd. Huntaway ?
Adj. 178 Bde. R.F.A.

WAR DIARY
or
INTELLIGENCE SUMMARY

Army Form C. 2118

1/8th Brigade R.F.A.
Commanded by Lt. Col. B.H. Gee R.F.A.

Folio 21

Place	Date	Hour	Summary of Events and Information	Remarks and references to Appendices
PHILOSOPHE	15th Oct 1916		Enemy T.M's again very active. Battery retaliated repeatedly, & carried out further registration. Barometer 29.8 Temperature 55°.	1/8th FA Bde adj
	16/10/16		Quiet day. Major G.H. Briggs R.F.A. assumes temporary command of Brigade vice Major Bawden sick. Barometer 30.1 Temperature 50.	1/8th FA Bde adj
	17/10/16		Quiet day. Barometer 30 Temperature 52 Wet.	1/8th FA Bde adj
	18/10/16		Enemy still very quiet. Very wet day. Barometer 30. Temperature 50. Major C.E. Massey 1/5 R.F.A. assumes temporary command of Brigade vice Major Briggs. Temperature 53°. Section still quiet. Barometer 29.8. Observation better.	1/8th FA Bde adj
	19/10/16		Still quiet. Clear cold day, observation excellent good. Barometer 29.9 Lt. Col. B.H. Gee returns from leave and resumes command of Bde. Thermometer 51.	1/8th FA Bde adj
	20/10/16			1/8th FA Bde adj
	21/10/16		Received T.M. activity in Section. Weather fair & cold. Barometer normal 2/Lt H.W. Briggs to C/181. 2/Lt. H.M. Horsfall from 6/181. Thermometer 36 Enemy T.M's exceptionally active. LEFT GROUP confirmed with 1/20th Jaquiri Br. in minor enterprise. Operation orders attached. Barometer 29.9 Thermometer 51.	1/8th FA Bde adj
	22/10/16			1/8th FA Bde adj
	23/10/16		Enemy T.M's again very active. Wet day. Barometer and thermometer 42 Major C.E. Vickery 1/5 R.F.A. assumes command of Brigade during absence of Lt. Col. Gee on shelled duty.	1/8th FA Bde adj

J. Vickery Major
1/5 R.F.A.
a/c 1/8 Bde R.F.A.

WAR DIARY or INTELLIGENCE SUMMARY

Army Form C. 2118

148th Bridge R.F.A.
Commanded by Lt. Col. S.H. Gee R.F.A.

Place	Date	Hour	Summary of Events and Information	Remarks and references to Appendices
PHILOSOPHE	25/10/16		Day quieter. Very wet, observation conditions bad. Barometer 29.7 Temperature 48	War Diary 148th Bde a/y
	26/10/16		Quiet day. Weather conditions bad. Barometer 29.4 Thermometer 49. 121st Infantry Brigade relieved 120th Infantry Brigade in HULLUCH SECTOR.	War Diary 148th Bde a/y
	26/10/16		Still quiet. D Battery practiced aeroplane co-operation. Results good. Weather conditions improved. Barometer 29.6 Thermometer 55.	War Diary 148th Bde a/y
	27/10/16		2/Lt. B.N. Buchman (S.R.) 2/Lt. P. E.T. Allen (S.R.) & 2/Lt. A. Reid (T.F.) posted from 2nd Division. Barometer 29.6 Thermometer 46 Weather conditions bad. Major Vickery departs to reform battery. H. Col. S.H. Gee returns from special duty.	War Diary 148th Bde a/y
	28/10/16		Batteries carry out Registration with aeroplane observation. Results moderate only, due to high wind. Barometer 29.6 Thermometer 52.	War Diary 148th Bde a/y
	29/10/16		Very quiet day. Wet and cold. Barometer 29.5 Thermometer 45.	War Diary 148th Bde a/y
	30/10/16		Still quiet. Wet and snow. Aircraft activity very high indeed. Barometer 29.5 Thermometer 49. Successfully quickened by Rapid burst of fire from about 2 mm.	War Diary 148th Bde a/y
	31/10/16		Stiles of night 16 record. Weather conditions brighter. Barometer 29.7 Thermometer 50.	War Diary 148th Bde a/y

Cartwright Lieut. R.F.A.
Adjutant 148th Brigade R.F.A.

SECRET   Copy No. 9.

[Stamp: 178TH BRIGADE ROYAL FIELD ARTILLERY]

LEFT GROUP OPERATION ORDER

Reference to Trench Maps 36c N.W.3
Edition 4.B.

1.   On the night of the 5th–6th October the 8th Division will be carrying out combined Gas attacks and Raids on the enemy trenches in H.13.c. and H.12.d.
   The Gas attacks will take place at ZERO time + 0.45 and + 2.30.
   The Raids at + 4.05.

2.   A party from the 125th Infantry Brigade will raid the enemy's trenches between H.31.b.15.60. and H.31.b.12.72. at + 5.58 on the same night. Gaps have been cut by French *

3.   The LEFT GROUP Artillery will co-operate and assist both enterprises as under:—

4.   During the day of the 5th October, A/178 will cut a gap in a spot to be selected between H.31.b.15.60. and H.31.b.12.72.
   The O.C. A/178 will arrange to place a gun in the position pointed out to him, during the night of the 4th–5th Octr. together with 300 rounds of "A" ammunition. The ammunition with bad fuzes to be used up. He will previously visit the O.C. 11th K.O.R. Lancs Regt. and arrange with the Officer who will be in charge of the raid, the exact spot for cutting the wire.

5.   The following points on which batteries will fire during the night of the 5th–6th Octr. will be registered by them not later than evening of 4th October.
   18-pdrs will fire AX only.
   A/178 Front Line BOMBARDMENT "A"
      H.31.b.20.23.
      H.31.b.20.36.
      H.31.b.18.50.
      H.31.b.12.60.
      H.31.b.12.68.
      H.31.b.10.78.
      BARRAGE "B"   H.31.b.20.23. (same as "A")
                     H.31.b.35.23.
                     H.31.b.40.25.   Ruined Houses
                     H.31.b.45.28.
                     H.31.b.40.65.
                     H.31.b.40.75.

* Mortars and Bangalore Torpedoes in the enemy's wire just N of Point 112.713, and it is hoped to convince the enemy that this will be the point raided.

Part II.   Art Group Operation Order   2/10/16

C/161   Front Line BOMBARDMENT "A"
          H. 31. b. 05. 96.
          H. 31. a. 99. 94.
          H. 25. c. 95. 05.
          H. 25. d. 00. 20.
          H. 25. d. 15. 21.
          H. 25. d. 25. 26.

        BARRAGE "B"
        1 gun on H. 31. a. 99. 94. (Same as "A")
        Remaining 5 guns barrage support trench
        H. 31. b. 36. 98 to H. 25. d. 35. 25. both points
        inclusive.

D/178   Front Line "A" 1 Howitzer on M.G. in Sap
        at H. 31. d. 05. 93.

        BARRAGE "B"
          H. 31. d. 05. 93. (M.G. in Sap)
          H. 31. b. 37. 10   (same as in Bomb. No 4.)
          H. 31. b. 65. 58.
          H. 31. b. 25. 90.

6.   Time Table and Rate of Fire.
          (All times from ZERO TIME)

     Hrs. Mins.

   + 5.   55.   A/178 C/161 fire at rate of 3 rounds per gun per
                   minute Front Line BOMBARDMENT "A" for 3 minutes.

                   D/178. One Howitzer on Sap at H. 31. d. 05. 93. at rate
                   of one round a minute for 3 minutes.

   + 5.   58.   A/178. C/161 fire at rate of 2 rounds per gun per
                   minute on BARRAGE "B" for 12 minutes.

                   D/178. fires at rate of 1 round per Howitzer per
                   minute on BARRAGE "B" for 12 minutes.

   + 6.   10.   A/178 C/161 and D/178 continue BARRAGE "B" at
                   rate of fire of one round per gun and howitzer
                   per minute for 10 minutes.

   + 6.   20.   A/178 and C/161 continue BARRAGE "B" at rate of
                   one round per gun every two minutes for
                   half an hour.

                   D/178 Two howitzers only continue firing on
                      H. 31. d. 05. 93. (M.G. in SAP) and
                      H. 31. b. 37. 10 at rate of one round per
                      howitzer every two minutes for half an hour.

   + 6.   50.   STOP FIRING.

   + 7.   35.   Every 18-pdr gun will fire one round on
                   Front Line BOMBARDMENT "A"
                         CEASE FIRING.

58th Div. 1st? Left Group Operation Order   2.9.16

The 6 inch Howitzer will fire one round every 3 minutes on TRENCH JUNCTION H.26.d.35.12 commencing at +5.55 and ceasing fire at +6.50.

7. C/178 will be kept in hand to fire on any possible counter attack on the LEFT Battalion front and will be ready to open fire at a moment's notice.

8. If wind &c. is unfavourable the operations may be postponed either until a later hour or until another day. The following Code will be used on the day of the 5th:—

   ZEPPELIN YORK   = Gas will be discharged at hours laid down.

   ZEPPELIN PORTSMOUTH = Gas attack postponed till tomorrow.

   ZEPPELIN MARGATE   = Gas discharge (i.e. ZERO time) will be changed from original time to
   *...........pm.   *........pm. and whole programme will be altered accordingly.

9. ZERO TIME will be communicated later to all concerned. Watches will be synchronised at 7 p.m. on the night of the 5th.

10. Sketch attached showing points to be registered for BARRAGE "B".

11. The following amounts of Ammunition will be expended:—

			A	AX	DX	F
B/178	Wire cutting		300			
	Bombardment	"A"		84		
	Barrage	"B"		144		
				60		
				60		
			300	348		
C/161	Bombardment	"A"		54		
	Barrage	"B"		144		
				60		
				90		
				348		
D/178	Bombardment	"A"			3	
	Barrage	"B"			48	
					40	
					30	
					121	
6 inch Howitzer						20
		Grand Total	300	696	121	20

SECRET.   Copy No. 9.

LEFT GROUP ORDER No 5.

Reference LOOS Map. 36°. N.W. 3.
Edition 1c.
October 20th 1916.

1. **Information.** The 4th H.L.I. will carry out a minor enterprise on the night of 22/23rd October 1916. They intend to enter the trenches at H.19.d.10.35 and H.19.d.02.50.
Their object is to cause losses to the enemy, to secure prisoners and identifications.

2. **Artillery Co-operation.** The Artillery will co-operate as under:-

    Wire Cutting. B/78 will cut the wire on the 21st at the two points of entry from a selected position which has been communicated to the O.C. B/78.
    On the 22nd, the gaps will be re-cut if they have been closed by the enemy.
    300 rounds "A" are allotted for the operation on the 21st, and 100 "A" for that of the 22nd.

3. **Barrage.** The Barrage points for guns participating in the enterprise and rate of fire, are as shown on attached TABLE "A".
The Barrage will be established at ZERO time and will last for 66 minutes, or until the Infantry are back from the raid.

4. **False Barrage.** On the 22nd TRENCH JUNCTION behind the enemy front line from H.19.a.75.48 to H.13.c.55.07 will be registered as if for a barrage, to deceive the enemy.

5. **Registration.** The switch to the real barrage can be worked out from the registration of points in enemy's lines between H.19.a.75.48 and H.13.c.55.07. The actual point for the Barrage will not be registered.

6. **Ammunition.** For wire cutting "A".
For the Barrage and dummy registration "AX".
The dummy registration will be carried out with the daily allotment of "AX".

7. **Zero.** ZERO time will be notified to an officer from each battery, who will attend at LEFT GROUP. Hd. Qrs at 4.30 p.m. on 22nd to synchronise watches.

8. **Code word.**   The code word for the operation
                    "PEREGRINE"

                              Trokeridge HBto
20/10/16   Major R.F.A.
                          Commanding LEFT GROUP

        Issued at   by Orderly G.
          Brys   No 1.
          Btys   2
          Btys   3
          60th A.A. 4
          120th Inf Bde. 5
          Centre Group   6
          Right Group   7
          R. Group 8th Div 8
          Etc.   10

TABLE 1

Series No	Battery	N° of guns	Major Commands	Rate of fire	Duration of Barrage	Expenditure (by series) A.A. 128	Expenditure (by series) A.A. 128
1	{C 275 Bty}	1	H. 19. o. 92. 70	18 pdrs 0. & 5. 3 rounds a gun a minute 4.5" & 6" 2 rounds a gun a minute Howitzers One round from every gun every two minutes.	140 minutes	125	60
2	{275 Bty}	1	H. 19. d. 10. 80			125	60
3	D/75	2	H. 19. d. 41. 51			250	—
4	{275 Bty}	2	H. 19. d. 26. 87			250	60
5	{275 Bty}	1 1	H. 19. d. 57. 29			125	60
						875	240

N.B. The Barrage is not intended to last full 60 minutes but allowance has to be made for first burst. The expenditure of ammunition is calculated on the basis of a 60 minute barrage.

U R G E N T   S E C R E T

S T R A F E - I N G.

1. There will be a combined strafe of the enemy's Front Line Trench from H.19.d.00.54 to H.19.c.94.79 tomorrow, 1st Novr. 1916. at 12.30.p.m.

2. D/178 will fire 80 rounds HX (20 rounds per Howitzer)

   2 Hows on Trench Junction at H.19.c.94.79.
   1 How.   H.19.c.93.75.
   1 How.   H.19.c.93.71.
   Rate of fire one round per Howitzer every 90 seconds.

   Two 6 inch Howitzers will fire 60 (or 40) rounds, 30 (or 20) rounds per Howitzer.

   One Howitzer on each of the Trench Junctions
            H.19.c.95.68.
            H.19.d.00.54.
   Rate of fire one round per Howitzer per minute.

   Four 60-pdrs will fire 60 rounds, that is, 15 rounds per gun on the Front Line Trench from H.19.c.95.68 to H.19.d.00.54.
   Rate of fire one round per gun every two minutes.

   B/178. (4 guns) will fire 100 rounds "A" ammunition,

   (Ammunition with bad fuses to be used only)
   that is, 25 rounds per gun on four points on the enemy's wire between H.19.d.00.54 and H.19.c.94.79.
   Rate of fire one round per gun per minute.

3. B/178. will register at 10.30.a.m.

   D/178   "   "   " 11.a.m.

   Heavy Artillery "   " 11.30.a.m.

4. Watches will be synchronised by telephone from these Head-Quarters at 10.a.m.

31/10/16.

Lt. Col. R.F.A.
Commanding L E F T   G R O U P.

WAR DIARY or INTELLIGENCE SUMMARY

(Erase heading not required.)

Army Form C. 2118

V-16
149th Brigade R.F.A.
Commanded by Lt. Col. D.H. Gee R.F.A.

FOLIO 23

Place	Date	Hour	Summary of Events and Information	Remarks and references to Appendices
PHILOSOPHE	1st April 1916	12·30 6·10 pm	B. & D. Batteries continued with Heavy Artillery carried out a shoot of the enemy's front line trench from H.19.d 00.54 to H.19.c 94.79. Enemy's trench was badly damaged, and was practically demolished. Weather fair. Barometer 30 The enemy retaliated on our front line in H.19.c. Thermometer 49	Reference Map 36 c N.W. 3 1/10000 Ed.7c Lieut ? R.F.A Adj.
	2/4/16		Exceedingly quiet day. Slight T.M. activity during the night. Weather improved Thermometer continues better. Barometer 29.8 Thermometer 52 2nd Lt. PRT ALLEN 8/178th posted to D/188. Temp Lieut W.J. Price from D/188 to B/178th	Lieut ? R.F.A Adj.
	3/4/16		C/178 carried out registration by aeroplane observation. Enemy's artillery slightly less active. Barometer 29.8 Thermometer 48 2nd Lt. W.N. Horsfield and T.M. Capt. R.N. Rutleigh granted leave to England. 2nd Lt. A. Stenhouse to C/178 from B/188.	Lieut ? R.F.A Adj.
	4/4/16		Conditions quite normal. Exceedingly high wind, but dry. Barometer 29.5 Thermometer 52	Lieut ? R.F.A Adj.
	5/4/16		Wind still very high. Rain. Barometer 29·1 Thermometer 54 Tactical situation quite normal.	Lieut ? R.F.A Adj.
	6/4/16		Weather conditions still very bad. Wind high, with rain. Barometer 29.14 Thermometer 49 Tactical situation very quiet.	
	7/4/16		Tactical situation still very quiet. Weather conditions unaltered. Wind storm. Barometer 29.3 Thermometer 46	Lieutenant C. ? R.F.A Adjutant. 1/4th Argyll R.F.A

WAR DIARY
or
INTELLIGENCE SUMMARY

(Erase heading not required.)

Army Form C. 2118

148th Brigade R.F.A.
Commanded by Lt. Col. D.H. Gull R.F.A.

Place	Date	Hour	Summary of Events and Information	Remarks and references to Appendices
PHILOSOPHE	8th Nov 1915		Hostile Artillery unusually active in HULLUCH SECTOR. Battery retaliation heavily. Weather conditions slightly improved. Barometer 29. Thermometer 50.	[initials] 148th R.F.A. Bde.
	9/11/15		Weather conditions much improved. C/178 cooperated with aeroplane in registration engaged with Heavy Artillery was evident to be a STORES DUMP. Enemy retaliated damage. Barometer 29.7 Thermometer 45	[initials] 148th R.F.A. Bde.
	10/11/15		Enemy very quiet. Weather conditions good. B/178 M cooperated with aeroplane in registration. Barometer 30.3 Thermometer 48.	[initials] 148th R.F.A. Bde.
	11/11/15		Quiet day. Weather conditions fair. Barometer 30.4 Thermometer 52.	[initials] 148th R.F.A. Bde.
	12/11/15		Quiet day. Weather conditions fine. Barometer 30.3 Thermometer 52.	[initials] 148th R.F.A. Bde.
	13/11/15		Enemy quiet. Battery cooperated with Heavy Artillery in a continued bombardment of the Enemy's trenches H.13.c. Copy of orders attached. Barometer 30.2 Thermometer 53.	[initials] 148th R.F.A. Bde.
	14/11/15		Hostile Artillery & T.M's more active. Enemy retaliation for yesterday's bombardment. Weather conditions good. Barometer 30.3 Thermometer 50.	[initials] 148th R.F.A. Bde.
	15/11/15		Enemy quiet. Weather dry & cold. Battery registration fresh bombardment arrange. orders attached. Barometer 30.4 Thermometer 35.	[initials] 148th R.F.A. Bde.
	16/11/15		Quiet day on both sides. Weather bitter dry & very cold. Barometer 30.2 Thermometer 33.	[initials] 148th R.F.A. Bde.

[signature] Lt Williams
148th Bde R.F.A.

WAR DIARY
or
INTELLIGENCE SUMMARY
(Erase heading not required.)

Army Form C. 2118

Folio 25

178th Bngde R.F.A
Commanded by Lt. Col. G.H. Gill R.F.A

Place	Date	Hour	Summary of Events and Information	Remarks and references to Appendices
PHILOSOPHE	17th Jan 1916		Tactical Situation very quiet. Continue canal and registration from new emulsion. Weather still wet and dry. Barometer 29.9 Thermometer 29.	Lieut. 178th R.F.A adj.
	18/1/16		Quiet day. Weather changed to rain / snow. Barometer 28.8 Thermometer 30.	Lieut. 178th R.F.A adj.
	19/1/16		Still quiet on our front. Lt Col. D.H. GILL assumes command of 178th Bde R.F.A for LT. Col. H.B. ALLEN R.F.A A.A. group 1st ARMY T.F. Thermometer 46	Lieut. 178th R.F.A adj.
	20/1/16		Quiet day. Weather brighter. Barometer 29.2 Thermometer 46	Lieut. 178th R.F.A adj.
	21/1/16		Enemy T.M. action during night, otherwise quiet. Barometer 29.4 Thermometer 37 Weather conditions dry + cold.	Lieut. 178th R.F.A adj.
	22/1/16		Quiet day. Nothing of interest to record. Barometer 29.8 Temperature 40 Weather bright. Fairly high wind.	Lieut. 178th R.F.A adj.
	23/1/16		Enemy artillery more active than usual. Weather conditions fair. Barometer 30.3 Thermometer 49	Lieut. 178th R.F.A adj.
	24/1/16		Quiet day. Weather conditions fair. Barometer 30.2 Thermometer 44	Lieut. 178th R.F.A adj.
	25/1/16		Still quiet. Considerable areal activity. Barometer 29.9 Thermometer 50	Lieut. 178th R.F.A adj.

Lt. Col. 178th R.F.A
Adjutant 178th Bde R.F.A

WAR DIARY
or
INTELLIGENCE SUMMARY
(Erase heading not required.)

Army Form C. 2118

178th Brigade R.F.A.
Commanded by Lt Col. H. B. ALLEN R.F.A. (T.F.)

FOLIO 26

Place	Date	Hour	Summary of Events and Information	Remarks and references to Appendices
PHILOSOPHE	26/11/16		Considerable aerial activity. D. Battery Position shelled with 5·9's. Enemy two casualties killed & wounded. Weather conditions good. Barometer 29.6 Thermometer 30.	Hwk 34/9/6 Adj.
	27/11/16		Enemy aeroplane still very active. Shots were dropped on D. Battery Position at 7.25 am causing 3 Casualties (wounded) Weather fair. Barometer 29.9 Thermometer 37	Hwk 34/9/6 Adj.
	28/11/16		Quiet day. Slight T.M. activity only. Observation any is met. Barometer 30.4 Thermometer 35	Hwk 34/9/6 Adj.
	29/11/16		Quiet day. Still misty + very cold. Lieut. A.N. OWEN proceeded to Report at SHOEBURYNESS on 3·12·16 Observation difficult owing to mist on Barometer 30·1 Thermometer 31	Hwk 34/9/6 Adj.
	30/11/16		Very Quiet day. Weather cold, raining. Observation conditions bad. Barometer 30.2 Thermometer 35	Hwk 34/9/6 Adj.

HB Allen Lt Col: R.F.A.
Commdg: 178th Brigade R.F.A.

SECRET.

MINOR OPERATION 12/11/16.

1. There will be a combined bombardment tomorrow, 13th Novr at 12 noon, of the enemy's Trench Junctions.

   H.13.c.65.82
   H.13.c.60.80.
   H.13.c.65.76.
   H.13.c.67.81.

2. The bombardment will last from 12 noon until 12.40.p.m.

   Six inch Howitzers will fire 40 rounds and 60-pdrs 60 rounds.

   D/178 will fire one round (BX) per Howitzer every two minutes

   C/178 (6 guns) will fire (AX) Battery fire 30 seconds interval.

3. Heavy Artillery will register between 10.30.a.m. and 12 noon.

   C/178 and D/178 will check their registrations before 10.30.am.

4. The LONE Howitzer will fire 30 rounds at the rate of one round per minute on the registered point H.13.c.72.13. commencing at 12 noon. Fire of this Howitzer to be observed and corrected when necessary.

5. Watches will be synchronised from these Headquarters at 11.a.m.

12/11/16.
                Lt. Col. R.F.A
Commanding LEFT GROUP. 40th Div. Arty.

Copies to   40th D.A.
            1st Corps H.A.
            72nd Infantry Bde.
            C/178
            D/178
            Officer i/c LONE How.
            File.

SECRET

To O.C. D/178th Bde. R.F.A.

Reference LOOS 36c N.W.3.
Ed. 7. c.

Please register the under mentioned Trench Junctions forming points of a box barrage.

1.
   H.19.a.82.51
   H.19.a.92.75
   H.13.c.89.12.   about
   H.13.c.70.15.

2. Ammunition to be used 20 rounds BX.

3. These registrations to be carefully noted for future use.

4. These are to be registered on the morning of the 15th Novr.   after 12 noon

5. Acknowledge receipt by wire.

                    [signature] Lt. Col. R.F.A.
                    Commanding LEFT GROUP.

14/11/16.

SECRET.

Reference LOOS 36c.N.W.3. Ed. 7.0.

O. C.
   B/178
   C/178
   72nd Infy. Bde.
   40th D.A.

       Please register the undermentioned front line bombardment and box barrage.

1.   B/178.   Front Line from H.19.a.75.47. to H.13.c.67.07.

2.   C/178.   Trench Junctions.

          H.19.a.82.51.
          H.19.b.03.56
          H.19.a.92.75
          H.19.a.95.87.
          H.13.c.69.12.
          H.13.c.70.13.

3.   Ammunition.   B/178 to use from 20 to 30 rounds "A"
                  C/178 "   "   30 to 50 "   "AX"

4.   These registrations to be carefully noted for future use.

5.   These are to be registered on the morning of the 15th Novr.

14/11/16.

                                Lt. Col. R.F.A.
                       Commanding LEFT GROUP.

WAR DIARY
or
INTELLIGENCE SUMMARY

Army Form C. 2118

T0/1/0
27

19th Brigade R.F.A.
Commanded by Lt. Col. H.B. Allen R.F.A. T.F.

Vol 7

Place	Date	Hour	Summary of Events and Information	Remarks and references to Appendices
PHILOSOPHE	1/12/16		Quiet day. Nothing of interest to record.	Lieut. H.R.A. Adj
	2/12/16		Slight activity by enemy's artillery in vicinity of HULLUCH CRATERS.	Lieut. H.R.A. Adj
	3/12/16		Hostile enemy artillery relieved by 34th Divnl. Artillery in HULLUCH SECTOR. 2 Sections each of A & C Batteries relieved 4 on section of D Battery. On being relieved sections marched to billets of LAPUGNOY.	Lieut. H.R.A. Adj
	4/12/16		Remaining sections of batteries relieved and march to LAPUGNOY. Reliefs completed by 8.0.pm when Bde. H.Q proceeded to LAPUGNOY.	Lieut. H.R.A. Adj
LAPUGNOY	5/12/16		Bgde rest at LAPUGNOY and fill up on echelon with ammunition.	Lieut. H.R.A. Adj
OSTREVILLE	6/12/16		Brigade marched to OSTREVILLE via DIVION – OURTON – DIEVAL. Weather conditions bad.	Lieut. H.R.A. Adj
VACQUERIE	7/12/16		Brigade marched to VACQUERIE. Weather conditions bad.	Lieut. H.R.A. Adj
AMPLIER	8/12/16		Brigade marched to AMPLIER via FREVENT – DOULLENS. Weather still bad.	Lieut. H.R.A. Adj
VILLERS BOCAGE	9/12/16		Brigade marched to VILLERS-BOCAGE via TALMAS.	Lieut. H.R.A. Adj
CAMP 114 NEAR BRAY	10/12/16		Bde. H.Q. A & B Batteries move into the line & march to Camp 114 near BRAY. A & B Batteries are accommodated in HUTS taken over from the relieved Batteries come under the orders of 33rd Divnl. Artillery.	Lieut. H.R.A. Adj

Lieutenant H.R.A.
Adj. 19 Bde. R.F.A.

Folio 28

WAR DIARY
INTELLIGENCE SUMMARY

Army Form C. 2118

14/8th Brigade R.F.A.
(Commanded by Lt. Col. H.B. Allen R.F.A. (T.F.))

Place	Date	Hour	Summary of Events and Information	Remarks and references to Appendices
CAMP 14 BRAY	11/12/16		A/178 march to Camp 20. war afterwards move into the line to relieve French battery of B.5.c. 95·85.	Reference Map ALBERT contoured 1/40000
- do -	12/12/16		B/178 march to Camp 17 war afterwards move into the line to relieve French battery at B.5.c. 95·90.	57 c SW 4 1/10000 62 C NW 2 1/10000 Army H.Q. Adv.
- do -	13/12/16		C/178 march to Camp 20. and afterwards move into the line to relieve French Battery at T.23.c.95·50. 1 Other wounded. Bde. H.Q. move to French H.Q. at B.11.d.3.7.	4 Div. H.Q. Adv.
NEAR COMBLE ARDERLU WOOD	14/12/16		D/178 move direct from Camp 14 into the line to relieve French battery at C.5.d.07.44. Relief completed. H.Q. & Regt. of Artillery depart.	4 Div. H.Q. adv.
- do -	15/12/16		Day devoted to settling into new positions. Great difficulty experienced in the supply of ammunition owing to the soft nature of the ground. Pack ammunition carriers used.	4 Div. H.Q. adv.
	16/12/16		Weather condition very bad. Considerable sickness among all ranks. Battery unable to carry out registration owing to mist.	4 Div. H.Q. adv.
	17/12/16		Weather still bad, very cold. Shelling by the enemy during the day. Intermittent.	4 Div. H.Q. adv.
	18/12/16		Weather slightly improved, but still extremely cold. Tactical situation normal.	
	19/12/16		Situation normal. Weather condition no change.	

Hutsurdyk
Adj 178th Bde R.F.A.

Army Form C. 2118

WAR DIARY
or
INTELLIGENCE SUMMARY
(Erase heading not required.)

Instructions regarding War Diaries and Intelligence Summaries are contained in F.S. Regs., Part II. and the Staff Manual respectively. Title Pages will be prepared in manuscript.

Place	Date	Hour	Summary of Events and Information	Remarks and references to Appendices
BOIS D' ANDERLU N° COMBLES	20/12/16		Day wet & cold. Normal amount of shelling by the enemy. H.E. Shrapnel and Tear Bombs directed to strongpoints. Tactical situation normal. Weather no change.	Work +++ PH4 adj
	21/12/16		Continuous carrying parties fm night to night. Enemy's communications. Wire strewn condition improved. Shelling as to Registered Coys.	Work +++ PH4 adj
	22/12/16		Heavy shell fire intermittent during the day. Snipers 5.9" & 4.2". Weather conditions much improved.	Work +++ PH4 adj
	23/12/16		Day quieter than usual. Weather bright & strenuous conditions quite good.	Work +++ PH4 adj
	25/12/16		Xmas day. Quiet fine weather, reasonable dry wind. Continuous fire sniper on enemy's communication during the day. Enemy which the 6/17 Bn Position driven attention. 1 O.R. wounded by M.G. our telephone dmgd	Work +++ PH4 adj
	26/12/16		Fairly quiet day. Usual night-firing carried out by batteries. Weather fair.	Work +++ PH4 adj
	27/12/16		Artillery activity on both sides normal. Weather bright & clear. Brigade proceeds to England to attend course of gunnery.	Work +++ PH4 adj
	28/12/16		Major H.E. Davidson 250 Bty assumes Command vice Lt. Col. W.B. Allen. 6/17 Bn shelled with Brigade during absence of Lt. Col. Allen. 2 Casualties. Enemy's gas shells during the night, 27-28.th. Badly shaken. B.H.Q. severely strafed Aug 10.	Work +++ PH4 adj

[signatures]

WAR DIARY
or
INTELLIGENCE SUMMARY

(Erase heading not required.)

Army Form C. 2118

178th Brigade R.F.A
Commanded by Major L.E.O. Saunton R.F.A

Folio 30

Place	Date	Hour	Summary of Events and Information	Remarks and references to Appendices
ANDERLU WOOD Nt COMBLES	29/12/16		Quiet day. Less Artillery Activity. Weather Conditions fair	Lieut. SHtte adj
- " -	30/12/16		Quiet day. Advance Party of 188th Bde. R.F.a arrive. Weather conditions fair Lieut. SHtte withdrawn from the line to Wagon Lines	Lieut. SHtte adj
- " -	31/12/16		Remainder of 178 withdrawn from the line & proceed to wagon lines. Brigade H.Q. of 188th Brigade arrive to take over from 178th Brigade R.F.a	Lieut. SHtte adj

Saunton
A/Lt Col
178th Brigade R.F.a

188 Bde R.F.A.
now
178 Bde R.F.A. Vol 8

WAR DIARY

1917

Jan. 1. Took over from 178 Bde R.F.A. the control of left Group, 40th D.A. Infantry composed of A/188, on front of R. Somme in E. of RANCOURT. – Relieved the R.F.A. Batt. left Bde. and ran supplements to enemy front line S.H. of ST. PIERRE VAAST WOOD from C.3.d.35.40 & C.2.b.99.35. – Hostile Arty 3 g on positions in the line A Bart C. – D/188 remaining at CAMP 14. – Relief took place as follows: A/188 relieved C/178 at FREGICOURT. – B.188 relieved 13.178 C/188 relieved D/178 at & FROGERLU WOOD. – H.Q. established at C.E. corner of road.

Jan. 2. Drew up scheme for linear offensive will defensive – for manning MAMELON O.P. – applied for supervision of DECHAUVILLE track at Battery positions. – Drew up night firing programme for Batteries.

3. Test an aeroplane photo & Batteries. – Brew material from DOMINO DUMP for improving Bty positions. – Drew up & sent out night firing programme & Batteries.

4. A quiet day – took still forwards in improving Bty positions, gun pits etc.

5. The O.C. had a conference of B.C. when various matters of administration and tactical work were discussed. – The Guardian & Forthcoming break up of the 188 Bde was gone into. –

6. Shoot with the Mayor Line at CAMP 21. In preparing, standing up being informed. machine guns used. also dying room and baths. Canteen being opened.
That RANCOURT is received from Infantry daily. – On receipt of these and yours of the Group force in current with the higher limit. Several downed. frequent follow up fire. – Howitzer Ammunition exceptional good. – A number of hostile aeroplanes over today, heavy shelled by our A.A. guns but shots were negative had. FREGICOURT and FROGERLU WOOD shelled today.

7. Drawing up schemes for installation & retaliation for shelling on Battalion front. – Reconnaissance of O.P.s in the "Thermometer Line". Every skilful COMBLES & FREGICOURT.

8. Tournai sustain sent in to R.F.E. material for carrying on improvement in Ennemies. Enemies aircraft etc.

9. Letter received for reorganisation of Brigade. The scheme to bring up of R. 188 Bde. A/188 goes to 14 HBde. 13/188 & C/188 & 2 Bty. D/188 to K. Thermometer Line. H.Q. remains intact for the present.
R.H.A. Bde. C/188 & 2 Bty.

M—

1917

Jan. 10. Preparing scheme for S.O.S. lines for the new Group shortly to be formed & submitting same for approval. Reporting on O.P. in INTERMEDIATE LINE – having received orders to construct MAMELON O.P. sporting a Lewis. S.O.7 PRIEZ FARM on Rocket Battery. Drawing up instructions as to LIAISON duties.

11. New Group now consist of B.C. D/173, 1°/3rd & 1°/57th Bde 45th Bde R.F.A. Enemy shelled round PRESICOURT and PRIEZ FARM. Improving system of telephone communication. Daily programme of Group shots drawn up. Sn final difficulty in discovering a suitable O.P. for Howitzers of Hem front line. Battery of Provisional telephone constantly to spread. Further shelling of PRIEZ FARM with 5.9c.

12. S.O.S. line for Hoit of K Group amended found to Batteries. Bde. fronts split up & schemes sent to Batteries. Testing over Ford station from R.A. H Group & arrangement made to man same. New line laid. Quiet day.

13. Conference of B.C.'s. Area of line of Bk of Group and of D.A. Reported on position of 1°/57th/185. Application made for Decauville Track for ammo supply of Batteries. COMBLES shelled with 5.9c. Some shelling along whole Bde. front.

14. VISUAL SIGNALS. Scheme sent out & free. Plentiful supply of R.E. material obtained. MAUREPAS. All Batteries registering men day art, gun pits & telephone system.

15. Reconnoissance of new position for 57th/185. Ammunition to R.A. a fairly quiet day.

16. Quiet day. Group H.Q. being enlarged and improved.

1917

Jan. 17. Preparing plans of S.O.S lines, showing Hows or enemy front line and sending same to Batteries - Sent revised areas of fire of D/178 & D.A. Day and night firing programme sent to all Batteries of the Group daily. Tested r Lillycurs also took report and ack of D.A. and enemy. Preparing scheme in case of Hostile attack or night of our front - Ordered from Bombardment "COUNTER PREP" "HMBER".

18. Conference of B.C's when all the points raised by G.O.C. R.A. at previous day were discussed. 2a him of 40th Div T.M's attacked to group for patterns. Arrangements made for the burying of the Occauville track to arm 3rd S.C. A. & B. 178 Batteries.

19. 2/Lieut COATES to leave for England - Allotting zones to Batteries of the group, Sandwithy & D.A.fr approval

20. Further conference of B.C. group on points raised by G.O.C. R.A. at conference of Group Commanders the previous day - Reconnaissance made for advanced O.P. in F.7/B.OO5 LANE. Arranged with LIEUT. WERRIDGE the taking over of the administration of 178th Bde R.F.A - Writing D.A. not reference the Suffield station on the Occauville system for supply of ammunition to the various Batteries of the Group.

21. Application made for forces to man the Corps O.P.

22. Arranged with 2/Lt DUDNEY (SURREY YEO) attached 40th K.D.H. for the general treatment, arbitrary locales the r: keeping a daily question the boys in the car and a weekly stat/ condition amoneth our the horses keepers in good condition. Enemy shelled B.H. position of C/178 with 5.9.

23. C/178 gun shelled with 5.9. 4.2. shrumer fact quiet day G.O.C. Group H.Q. in being started improved a Cupola dugout being dug - receive some telephone lines laid out, other lines foreted - Rend stations being formed.

AKk

1917

Jan. 24 All work in connection with improvement of gunpits, dugouts, ammunition dumps, telephone lines being carried out. Fair quiet day.

25. In communication with D.A. and O.C. Right Group re introduction for 28th of enquiry return of the Sanitary & Battery concerned. A special record of GAS SHELL being drawn by 57th 185 and D/178. has on being kept apart from the other ammunition.

26. Lt. O.C. interviewed the following candidates for commissions from the ranks. No. S-160 Cr. B.S.M. GOODWIN G. A/178. 34173 Br BARNES H.C. A/178. 50647 BQMS HARPER G. B/178. L.29465. B°M°GREGOR W.J. D/178.

27. Col CAMPBELL (O.C. 46ᵗʰ Bde) arrived and visited all the Batteries with O.C. also Infantry Battalion J.H.Q. Enemy shewed its actions and inactivation with a view to working our Firemen.

28. Handed over command of Left Group to Col CAMPBELL. reported completion of relief to 40ᵗʰ D.A. and to 6ᵗʰ D.A. 178 H.Q. Staff moved to Kayan Linn Camp 25. home of St BARNES and BQMS HARPER forwarded and recommended for Commissions.

29. Riding with administration matters of the Bde. house

30. home of A/CAPT PRICE and A/CAPT BAVICTER recommended for acting Commissions. Application for making in leave have had, all the three have been to go to SOZANNIS for work. there is no place round them not frozen up.

31. LT COL PARSONS left for England on leave. MAJOR L.F.O. DAVIDSON D.S.O in command of the Bde.

FEB. 1 R.S.M. McLELLAN Commissioned forwarded to report to 50ᵗʰ D.H. C/178 Rott and their gun hauled then to position was MARRIER/WOOD Officers + men returned to Camps 21.

W. Williamson
Major R.F.A.
f° O.C. 178ᵗʰ Bde R.F.A

178 Bde R.F.A.

Vol 9

1917
Feb 1. R.S.M. McLELLAN commissioned and proceeded to report to 50th D.A. — C/178 stk out their guns landed them to a position near MARRIERES WOOD Officers' men returned to Camp 21.

Feb 2. Gun detachment of C/178 relieved & passed by both teams to VAUX sur SOMME. The following names and forward for foreign decoration. MAJOR S.M. NOAKES — TEMP. CAPT.
   H.B. BAVINTER.   B.S.M. GODWIN (A/178)

3. Recommendation of B.Q.M.S. HARPER for permanent Armourer forwarded —
   A case of Contagious Stomatitis has occurred in D/178 horse lines, isolation troughs have been arranged & stable disinfected.

4. Name of LT WEEKES submitted for appointment as instructor at 1st Army School —

5. Justice case of Stomatitis — been received in D/178. Everything still frozen up, horses lame.

   K 2, L SUZANNE for stables.

6. Br CHADWICK B.H.Q. Staff recommended for Temp Comdr & attached to B/178 under instruction. Received from truck 178 Bde strong Vehicle. 9 £ 37. 16. 6.

7. Orders received from A.D.V.S. for the cleaning out and disinfection of horse troughs on account of Contagious Stomatitis — There is being carried out.

8. 9 horses purposing in improvement of horse lines, stabling and mens billets.

10. Receipt for hire and purchase of Chaff Cutter returned to Battn. received with Authority to purchase. There has disposed of.

11. Arrangement made with Corps for Motor lorries to fill isolation troughs —
    Brigade H.Q. Staff engaged every day on Telephony, Signalling by day and night. Superseding etc.

12. COL. PARSONS returned from leave & took on Temp Command of 40th D.A.

13-14-15. Work still proceeding on general improvement of horse lines. R.E. brickwork in bog drawn from dump near BRAY — The health of the men is greatly improved —

1917
Feb 15.   The Divisional Commander visited Camps 21 and made an inspection of men's quarters.

16.   Ammunition dumps at PLATEAU SIDING fired by enemy aeroplane at 4.30 a.m. The fire burnt all day and shell continued exploding. Keus sent in, fed up & to present an order to adopt Keus precaution.

17.   All men in boys lines are being again inoculated. The following recommendation put forward for promotion.

18.   Reported on the cutting Hd of stores supply – All the horses still here to g. to SUZANNE for watering – lines H. Those sent on the Camp is first drowning a Gregson yarn.

19.   Gas Bombardment and to revised Officer to A.R.P. "Keus precaution" are now in force. Summary of Evidence taken in case of Dr NODDCOCK 15/178 remanded for F.G.C.M.

20.   MAJOR RASHLEIGH and MAJOR DAVIDSON proceeded to England on 15% Commander leave. LT. COL ALLEN arrived and took over as O.C. 40th Div. boys line. 1 section of C/178 went into action in old position at FREGICOURT, another sector given us at 21st and last section on night 9.22nd.

21.   Still endeavouring to get works turned on to Camps 20 and 21. Instruction given for improvement to be carried out to rooms of the stretchers.

22.   Lot. Parsons took over from left Surg. 6th D.A. and reported relief. There is no tactical control however on the Camps of 7 a.m. on 23rd. Orderly Officer sent in horse to PARIS.

23.   Administration of the Army carried on from our H.Q.

24.   LT. McCABE and N.C.O from C/178 proceed on a course of Enemy ammunition (New) at VAUX-en-AMIÉNOIS.

Feb. 25. The 106 fuze are being used by the F.D.s. hun today for wire-cutting in front of FRITZ TRENCH. Wire is being opened to PARIS for 3 days for Officers, N.C.Os and men.

26. Weather conditions have been too adverse for the past week for any registration. But this afternoon observation conditions were good and batteries were busy registering and wire cutting.

27. Conference of Battery Commanders to discuss the return of the forthcoming move of the Brigade to positions S. of the SOMME.
Names submitted for honours last in follows. 2/Lt. F.W.G. COOK for Military Cross — LT. H.W. MANN
(adjutant) 2/Lt. J.M.B. HOMFRAY (Orderly Officer) MAJOR L.E.O. DAVIDSON for "Mention"
Sergt. J.H. BULLOCK A/178. Cpl. White. G.F. DEWEY B/178. Gnr. E. THOMAS. C/178. Cpl. H.H. HINE B.H.Q. Staff
for "Military Medal" Cpl. R.S. MAYO D/178. Dr. R. DALLISON C/178. Gnr G. PANKHURST B/178. Dr J.W. SEXTON
B/178. "Mention".

28. At 4.30 a.m. continuing with c.a.c. bombardment by French Div. supported by 40th D.F. Gorps followed by an attack on positions of enemy front line N. of PAILLISEL.

H.J. Amoore Lt.Col.

WAR DIARY

178 Bde R.F.A. Vol 10

March 1.2.3 — The Brigade is still under the Right Group 40th D.A. under the tactical control of Lt. Col. CAMPBELL.

4 — 8th Div supported by 40th D.A. Bombarded and afterwards captured FRITZ TRENCH and Trenches adjacent which commanded the open about the ford of the Somme. — Several counter attacks were made, but the new ground taken was held. 2/Lt MALTBY acting as F.O. was wounded.

5-6 — Everything very quiet — no further attempt by the enemy to recover lost ground.

7 — Rear Bty positions reconnoitred S. of the SOMME near BUCCOURT.

8-9 — Nothing of note happened.

10 — Bde. H.Q. moved to BUCCOURT. An Intel. mess from 33rd D.A. Gen plan BPK Bty forming the Right Group 40th D.A. Tak. over from Majr BELGRAVE A/178 on return N. & K. near by JUNCTION WOOD. B/178 at H.23.c.3.6. with a detached Xn. by K. near at H.17.a.38.85. C.178 adjoining B.H.Q. with a detached Xn. at H.28.c.3.6. D/176 H.23.a.3.6. with a detached Xn. adjoining C/176. and 22nd Bty also adjoining. O.P. established.

11 — Arrangements made to have the Battery Commanders in turn at Infantry Brigade and a Liaison Officer with Right and Left Battalions, also an O.P. with each Battery. Reported on all those taken over from 33rd Divn.

12 — Exploration party forward to see Canal for ammunition supply. Diagrams of O.P.s Lines & Punishment obtained forwarded to D.A.

13 — Infantry fired S.O.S. rockets from a pre-list for first time. Very successful.

14 — Sergt Bullock & Sergt Wilson departed to England to take up commissions. 188 & Bde H.Q. staff absorbed in the 178th Bde H.Q. Staff. Lt. Col. H.B. Allen posted to command # 7 D.A.

Mar. 15. 2/Lt DEARDON posted as Orderly Officer to Bn Brigade – 2/Lt HOMFRAY to 18/178.
Brevet of 188 H.Q. Staff posted to 17/8·B.H.Q. Lieut MITCHELL and Lieut JEFFRIES Commissioned.
A quiet day – Enemy Infantry carried out some rapid rifle fire with distilling acquisition, but a smear of
strong the enemy – the replied rather feebly with M.G. fire.

16. Another quiet day.

17. The enemy withdrew from front line opposite Right Bde first and our troops occupied PERLY BULGE
and front line S.E. of SOMME, outposts pushed out and soon crossed the S. and entered HALLE.
Bn. P. on Hounslow Ballons successfully attacked by three aeroplanes.

18. Enemy withdrew from FEUILLAUCOURT. MT ST QUENTIN. RADEGONDE. PERONNE. BUSCU. MOISLAINS.
HAUT ALLAINES. He is burning Villages in his retreat. Blowing up bridges and dumps.

19. Bn supports him withdraw to Rd when line P. Village. In hopes the enemy who first line in main line
of resistance.

20. Moved forward advanced B.H.Q. to HALLE at I.10.a.0.5. Battalion in action at A/178 T.19.6.9.5.
B/178 I.13.d.9.7. C/178 T.20.a.0.7. D/178 T.19.6.6.1. Outposts line HAUT ALLAINES. MT
St QUENTIN. PERONNE.

21. Our outposts have again pushed forward. Battalion in attack front line of moisture remain the same
Le which of B.H.Q. moved up to MT ST QUENTIN at I.16.a.2.2. Battalion moved forward front out
action as follows. A/178 I.17.c.4.9. B/178 I.16.a.2.3. C/178 I.22.b.44. D/178 I.22.a.7.7.
Outposts line E. of BUSCU   all Bde Hdqrs now at HALLE.

MNK

March 23. O.C. Bde. reconnoitred forward position at ORIENCOURT and Bty Commanders.

24. Bm. action B/178 and one section D/178 moved forward to join Mobile Column under Major McGOWAN

25. 2/Lt W. ROBINSON T.F. 2/Lt R.H. PAYNE T.F. 2/Lt R. SAWYER T.F. joined R. Bde.
    O.C. Bde. again reconnoitred forward to ORIENCOURT — MAJOR LLOYD attached 1st 2nd K.O.H. for instruction. Detached section rejoined R. Bde.

26. 2k Bde. marched to COMBLES and in temporary under 20k Div.

27. 2k O.C. Bde reconnoitred — with Bty Commanders — for position near ETRICOURT.

28. B/178 (with 4 guns) went into action at V.13.d.6.2. with W7a7 km. close by — D/178 (4 guns) went into action at V.13.d.3.9. Bde. H.Q. moved up to LE MESNIL at V.6.a.4.4. Brigade Comm. adjoining Bde. H.Q.

29. F/178 went into action at V.1.b.6.6. with W.L. at V.S.a.3.5. C/178 went into action at V.2.c.3.6. with W.L. at V.S.c.6.9.   O.C. Bde. reconnoitred for forward position for B and D Batteries.

30. 10th Rifle Bde. supported by R.A. Group established themselves on the line DESSART WOOD. W.1.c.0.8.
    P.24.c.o.o.   1 section B/178 went forward at V.9.b.9.3. and 1 section D/178 went forward to V.9.d.9.3.
    106 Remounts handed over to R. Bde.

31. B.H.Q. moved forward to ETRICOURT V.8.a.7.6..   Remaining sections of B & D/178 moved to forward position.

W.H. Brown Lt Col.
1st/178 Bde R.F.A.
Cmdg 1/178th Bde R.F.A.

WAR DIARY or INTELLIGENCE SUMMARY

Army Form C. 2118

178th Bde RFA

Place	Date	Hour	Summary of Events and Information	Remarks and references to Appendices
	Apl. 1		One of our observation balloons brought down by hostile aeroplane in neighbourhood of LE TRANSLOY. Another enemy plane dropped bombs in vicinity of Bde. H.Q. The Bde. Gen'l reconnoitred for Btys. position near FINS.	
	2		A/178 moved forward to position at V.6.6.2.5. B/178 to W.1.6.7.5. Enemy planes again dropped bombs near Bde. H.Q. – Bde. Gen'l 2nd horses and orderlies killed, 2 gunners wounded & 2 horses wounded by 4.2 near FINS.	
	3		Bde H.Q. and Bn. moved up to V.4.c.9.4. Road B began here to EQUANCOURT Bryn line to ETRICOURT. C/178 went into action at P.34.c.3.1. Enemy shelled vicinity of Bde H.Q. with 5.9. 2 horses killed & wounded. 20th Div supported by 40th D.A. Captured MET2. Battery opened at 2 p.m. at objective gained. Bde. Gen'l reconnoitred for new H.Q. and Batty positions.	
	4		D/178 went into action at W.1.c.4.0 and moved then began line to EQUANCOURT. Bde H.Q. moved to V.6.d.0.7. – Lt. SOUTHGATE in man team.	
	5		C/178 moved into action at W.1.a.7.7. – Enemy shelling rather than normal in vicinity	
	6		of DESSART WOOD. Both day and night.	
	7		A/178 moved into action at W.2.a.7.5 — wk reconnoitring party in GOUZEAUCOURT WOOD new O.P. established in Q.32.a. and 33.c. – 2/Lt FORD on various recon.	

WAR DIARY
or
INTELLIGENCE SUMMARY
(Erase heading not required.)

Army Form C. 2118

Place	Date	Hour	Summary of Events and Information	Remarks and references to Appendices
	9.4.17.		The 21st MIDDLESEX pushed outpost to X Roads on high ground at Q.23.c.7.2. and Q.23.a.9.1 under a particular barrage from 178 Bde R.F.A. Their post was consolidated with very few casualties. The night was quiet.	
	10th		Owing to the shelling of Farm in Q.32.d. (used as an O.P.) O.P.s were established at Q.32.d.9.7. and Q.32.c.8.9. also in a Tree in DESSART WOOD.	
	11		An O.P. was reconnoitred in HAVRINCOURT WOOD about Q.15.d.6.7 and a wire laid to same. From this O.P. observation can be obtained of ridge about Q.17.	
	12.		A very quiet day.	
	13.		In conjunction with 8th Div. on our right (who have reoccupied GOUZEACOURT and GAUCHE WOOD) and 20th Div. on our left (who have pushed forward in a N.E. direction through HAVRINCOURT WOOD) the 21st MIDDLESEX advanced their posts to X Road in Q.23.b. to Trench in Q.23.a. and b. and to Q.24.c.4.2. A medium barrage was placed during the advance and very little opposition was encountered.	
	14		Horses were moved up to horses in EQUANCOURT Sunken road for safety. Horses are being grazed daily.	
	15		O.C. reconnoitred for forward Battery position and O.P. in GOUZEACOURT WOOD and vicinity. F/178 went into action at Q.22.d.6.2.	

WAR DIARY
or
INTELLIGENCE SUMMARY

Army Form C. 2118

Place	Date	Hour	Summary of Events and Information	Remarks and references to Appendices
	4/16.		A very quiet day. Trench was dug last night by the Brigade to a forward O.P. on the crest at Q.23.a. — Gun of an stationary balloons on EQUANCOURT was brought down by an enemy plane.	
	17th		LT GRAHAM proceeded on leave to ENGLAND — Battery position is being moved in. D/178 moved forward to Q.28.a.0.3 (GOUZEACOURT WOOD) O.C. Bde. gave a lecture to Officers and Senior N.C.Os on "Horse management" — Lunch & O.P. completed. R.S.M. GILKS posted in probation from 8th D.A.C.	
	18th		The day was quiet, very little hostile shelling. A/178 was shelled with pinpoint quick in the evening.	
	19th		C/178 moved up to Q.34.a.1.8 (GOUZEACOURT WOOD) — METZ shelled this morning with 4·2 and 5·9c.	
	20th		Bde. H.Q. moved up to DESSART WOOD — W.1.t.1.6. — B/178 moved to W.4.d.1.5 and went into action.	
	21st		Infantry attack on defences of BEAUCAMP. All objectives gained. B/178 moved to new position in HAVRINCOURT WOOD at night. Q.15.c.0.7.	
	22		A very quiet day —	
	23rd		Bde H.Q. moved up to sunken Road Q.27.c.6.2.	

WAR DIARY
or
INTELLIGENCE SUMMARY

Army Form C. 2118

Place	Date	Hour	Summary of Events and Information	Remarks and references to Appendices
	Apl 24th		BEAUCAMP and VILLERS PLOUICH attacked at dawn by 120 Infantry Bde. supported by 40th D.A. Enemy was forced clear of 4.15 a.m. The night of the attack met with little opposition and soon gained all objectives, but the left were hung up by a counter attack, on Targon, just through the village, but forced enemy withdrew to a line just South of the village. About 650 prisoners were captured by us in the course of the operations. The infantry consolidated casualties in enemy reinforcement and digging position.	
	25.		Attack on BEAUCAMP resumed at 4.15 a.m. To find down a heavy cover which our Troops (120 Bde.) entered BEAUCAMP and gained all their objectives N. of the village and consolidated them.	
	26th		Enemy shelled 60 Pr Battery on outskirts of METZ with S.9c throughout most of the day but no damage was done to the Battery *. Great aerial activity - 2 of our machines driven down by the enemy - many observation balloons up on either side. * An ammunition dump was sent up by fire from S.9c. Enemy evidently expected an attack on it shelled all along our front at dawn.	
	27		121 Inf Bde relieved the 120 Inf Bde.	

WAR DIARY
or
INTELLIGENCE SUMMARY
(Erase heading not required.)

Army Form C. 2118

Place	Date	Hour	Summary of Events and Information	Remarks and references to Appendices
	Apr 28th		A/178 were shelled from 2 pm to 6 pm with 5.9" and suspected 8" - 150 rounds were sent over. An ammunition dump blown up, and 2 men slightly hurt in the gun slightly damaged. No casualties.	
	29th		Fairly quiet day. Great aerial activity. Gun positions of A, B and C/178 moved up. R.25.b.1.3. - R.19.c.9.3. - R.19.d.1.6. - Capt RICARDO Comd 92nd Bde called with No. 4 Bty Commander regarding an impending attack on LA VACQUERIE. Forward Bty positions with a view to taking over the work established. Our H.Q. at B/84 Position in HAVRINCOURT WOOD.	
	30		D/178 moved up towards to GOUZEACOURT Q.30.d.2.8. — 18 pdr Battery. A Battery in front of VACQUERIE. F Battery position again shelled with 5.9 and 4.2. One man wounded. 2/Lt STEPHENS A/178 slightly wounded.	

H.O. Armand Lt Col
Cmdg 178 Bde RFA
1/5/17.

WAR DIARY
or
INTELLIGENCE SUMMARY
(Erase heading not required.)

Army Form C. 2118

178 Bde R.F.A. May 1917

Place	Date	Hour	Summary of Events and Information	Remarks and references to Appendices
1.5.17	1.5.17		B/178 moved into GOUZEAUCOURT at night. Great hostile aerial activity. Five men in B/178 Rt. by the Enemy Shelling.	
2.5.17	2.5.17		Reconnoitred position of new H.Q. in Q.23.c. B/178 shelled by 4.2. 115th Btty shelled in the afternoon. No damage done. Shelled again in the evening. Q.M.S. was Rt.	
	3.5.17		Enemy Artillery active during the day. Major Rackleigh A/178. Slightly wounded, otherwise quiet.	
	4.5.17		Wire cutting continued. Practice Barrage from 4.5 a.m. to 4.17 a.m. Major Lloyd Rueward.	
	5.5.17		Wire cutting. Chinese Barrage from 4 a.m. to 4.12 a.m. Extensive raid on LA VACQUERIE at 11 p.m. Battle H.Q. at Q.29.a. 2.1. Barrage from 11 p.m. to 12.30 p.m. operation not entirely successful owing to heavy enemy barrage. Some prisoners were taken.	
	6.5.17		H.Q. reestablished at Q.27.c.4.3. 251st Bde R.A. moved out to rejoin 1st Divn.	
	7.5.17		Colonel reconnoitred battery positions near GOUZEAUCOURT WOOD. Some section of B/178 moved into vacated position of 115 Btty. at Q.22.c.3.8. A/178 came under the control of the Rt. Group and one section of C/178 moved to Q.20.c.5.5. These moved in order to cover the readjusted front of Left Bde, which now extends from R.7.t. 5.9. — Q.11. & 27.	
	8.5.17		Remaining sections of A + C/178 moved into new positions. 4 guns of B/178 estab'd into position at Q.22.c.7.7. O.P's were established at Q.23.A.8.8. Q.16.d. 3.4. Q.18. P.3.1. Guns were changed during this move with the 181 Bde R.F.A. in order to adjust the Calibration error of Batteries.	
	9.5.17		One of our aeroplanes brought down in Q.19.a. by Hun aeroplane at 1.10 p.m. New forward Telephone exchange established in GOUZEAUCOURT WOOD.	
	10.5.17		A Balloon strafe was arranged along the 4th Army front — The Hun however put no Balloons up for two days and so it fell flat. Our fight between 5 Huns and six of our planes	

WAR DIARY or INTELLIGENCE SUMMARY

(Erase heading not required.)

Army Form C. 2118

Place	Date	Hour	Summary of Events and Information	Remarks and references to Appendices
	11.5.17.		False gas alarm through Battalion transmitting message wrong. B. rc 1/78 fired on S.O.S. lines for 6 mins. rapid fire.	
	12.5.17.		Colonel reconnoitred positions of 45th Bde R.F.A. near VILLERS-GUISLAIN. from whom we take over. One of our aeroplanes was winged by a Hun Archie, and descended near NURLU.	
	13.5.17. 14.5.17.		Quiet day. One section from each Btty. in the Bde. took over from the gth Div. Bttries (45th Bde.) whose front we now cover.	
	15.5.17.		Remainder of the Batteries completed relief of 45th Bde. in conjunction with the 181 Bde. who also relieved on this front.	
	16.5.17.		2/Lt HERRDEN proceeded to LESQUESNOY to 4th ARMY SCHOOL OF SIGNALLING on a Course of Instruction. 2/Lt. K. HOLMES-TARN took over as Orderly officer to-day.	
	17.5.17.		An O.P. from which HONNECOURT could be seen was reconnoitred for B/178. by Capt. H.B.EMERTON. This was not achieved but an O.P. was selected in X.10.d. 55.85 which gave a good view of the surrounding country.	
	18.5.17 19.5.17.		Major WEBB (B/181) was killed to-day at 4.13 p.m. NYP. Two Hun planes attacked 5 of our. One was brought down in flames. Both occupants killed. At 3.45 p.m. Hun attacked the o.Balloon at RAILTON. but missed it. Both occupant came down in parachutes and landed safely. Man got away unhurt.	
	20.5.17.		Enemy plane was brought down at TRESCAULT.	

WAR DIARY
or
INTELLIGENCE SUMMARY

Army Form C. 2118

(Erase heading not required.)

Date	Hour	Summary of Events and Information	Remarks and references to Appendices
21.5.17.		Hun shelled the balloon at RAILTON and burnt it. The balloon was on the ground. No effort apparently was made to save it, although the Hun fired about 20 rounds or more before he hit it.	
22.5.17.		At 12.10 a.m. our Infantry carried out a small raid on Enemy lines. Artillery fired a barrage for 3/4 of an hour. F/178 had an accident with a gun. The breech complete blew off. One man GNR. SMITH was killed three others wounded, two severely. New Bde. H.Q. and Forward Exchange prepared. Quiet day.	
23.5.17.		Enemy abnormally quiet.	
24.5.17.			
25.5.17.		F/178 + C/181 shelled by 5.9's from 12.30 p.m. to 2.30 p.m. 150 rds. fired approx. One Section per Btty. moved into new positions, which with the exception of C were those of 181 Bde.	
26.5.17.		H.Q. completed move to W.10. Relief of Btties. complete by midnight.	
27.5.17.		Hun shelled W. of GOUZEAUCOURT from 7 a.m. till 1 p.m. 5.9's fired.	
28.5.17.		F/178 had 10 rds of 5.9's put over. Shining them ceased. One balloon up ably observing. WAGON LINES of the Bde. commenced to move from EQUANCOURT to W.8.	
29.5.17.		Move of Wagon lines A.B its complete by noon. C/178 move unexpectedly by 31st. New position reconnoitred by Colonel.	
30.5.17.		Very quiet day. Major RASHLEIGH F/178 awarded D.S.O.	
31.5.17.		Quiet day.	

H.H. Tudor Lt. Col.
Comdg 178th Bde R.F.A.
31/5/17.

WAR DIARY

INTELLIGENCE SUMMARY
(Erase heading not required.)

Army Form C. 2118

178 Bde R.F.A.

June 1917.

Vol 13

Place	Date	Hour	Summary of Events and Information	Remarks and references to Appendices
	1/6/17		Visual Signalling test: not very successful on the Battn. Fronts were badly aligned	
	2/6/17		C/178 shelled fairly heavily with 5.9's for about 5 hours: one gun damaged + camouflage burnt	
	3/6/17		B/178 shelled with 5.9's biggest part of the day: one gun knocked out. West end of GONZECOURT shelled with 5.9's, also Sqt OP. Batn. H.Q. & the 181 R.F.A. H.Q.	
	4/6/17		Enemy quieter: A and B Batteries lightly shelled.	
	5/6/17		Quiet day. combined shoot by B & D.178 on unshooted O.P at R.28.A.5.8.0 which succeeded in dislodging the Huns.	
	6/6/17		Enemy shelled GONNELIEU + in the afternoon obtained a direct hit on D/178 O.P. Lt. H. Neaves was slightly wounded + one telephonist badly wounded. Unsuccessful visual regarding test carried out in the evening.	
	7/6/17		Quiet day.	
	8/6/17		Quiet day.	
	9/6/17		Quiet day.	
	10/6/17		Unsuccessful shoot on enemy T.M. at R.28.A. commencement of relief of battalions in the line.	
	11/6/17		Relief completed. Battalions in the line :- N/. Battn. 12th Suffolks, Sth/Bttn. 20 Middlesex	

1875 Wt. W593/826 1,000,000 4/15 J.B.C. & A. A.D.S.S./Forms/C. 2118.

WAR DIARY
INTELLIGENCE SUMMARY
(Erase heading not required.)

Army Form C. 2118

178 R.F.A.   JUNE 1919.

Place	Date	Hour	Summary of Events and Information	Remarks and references to Appendices
	12/6/17		Quiet day.	
	13/6/17		Visual station manned for the first time by night, & a successful test carried out.	
	14/6/17		Quiet day.	
	15/6/17		A/178 shelled by 5.9 gun & abandoned position; no damage to guns or personnel. B/178 also shelled with 8" & abandoned position; no damage to guns or personnel.	
	16/6/17		A & B/178 lightly shelled in the morning; at 8.30 p.m. an enemy balloon went up over LA VACQUERIE & after ranging with this, started firing battery fire 3 secs & continuous fuses until 9.30 p.m. on both batteries; 3 guns put out of action; A/178 moved to new position at R.31.A.1.7.	
	17/6/17		Successfully "striped" a T.M. at R.26.A. Capt Cook C/178 R.F.A. presented with M.C. & Sgt Bullock A/178 with D.C.M. by Gen. Nicholson R.A.	
	18/6/17		Enemy artillery active - but no shelling on batteries.	
	19/6/17		Very quiet day.	
	20/6/17		Lt. Col. Parsons D.S.O. R.A. returned from leave.	
	21/6/17		FINS shelled this morning with 8". Successful visual signalling test carried out.	

Army Form C. 2118

WAR DIARY
or
INTELLIGENCE SUMMARY
(Erase heading not required.)

178 RFA   JUNE 1917

Place	Date	Hour	Summary of Events and Information	Remarks and references to Appendices
	22/6/17		Very quiet day	
	23/6/17		ditto.	
	24/6/17		Quiet day: about 8.10 p.m. enemy plane came over & attacked our O.B at HEUDECOURT: unsuccessful, through the observer took to his parachute. T.M. at 2.28 A.M. active; ordered "CAT" at 11.38 A.M. effective.	
	25/6/17		Hostile shelling below normal: 9.40 p.m. enemy plane over wagon lines & dropped a bomb near D Battery & another one near 178 Bde. H.Q.	
	27/6/17		Hostile shelling normal: 23 rds 5.9's on GOUZEAUCOURT STN. 23 enemy planes over during day. Both Infantry Battalions in line were relieved.	
	28/6/17		GONNELIEU had 120 5.9's during day; thunderstorm at 8.10 p.m. By in line :- Right battalion 18th Welch, Left Batn. 12th S.W. Borderers.	
	29/6/17		GOUZEAUCOURT and GONNELIEU and our front line at R.27.C. heavily shelled.	
	30/6/17		Quiet day: at 12 p.m. left battalion sent through "S.O.S." & we fired for 20 min. it transpired however, that a sentry saw the Huns send up 2 similar rockets to our S.O.S: whole thing a washout.	

H Stonehouse 2nd RFA
For Lt. Col. Comdg. 178 Brigade R.F.A

WAR DIARY
or
INTELLIGENCE SUMMARY
(Erase heading not required.)

Army Form C. 2118

Place	Date	Hour	Summary of Events and Information	Remarks and references to Appendices
In the Field	1-7-17		Enemy Artillery active. Our F.O.O. reported a relief taking place in R.22.A. at 1.47 A.M. Right Batn. sent through an S.O.S. We fired for 10 minutes but on further investigation S.O.S. proved to be unjustified their Left Company Commander on approach saw S.O.S. wash go up on his extreme right. Aerial activity, nil.	
	2-7-17		12.35 p.m. one of our planes brought down by E.A. & fell just N. of C/178 W.L. On the afternoon an E.A. attacked our balloon at HEUDICOURT but failed to hit it: The E.A. was brought down by M.G. fire & fell at N.W. end of HEUDICOURT.	
	3-7-17		Enemy Artillery active: much aerial activity.	
	4-7-17		Quiet day: nothing to report.	
	5-7-17		2/Lt DEARDEN returned from 6 week's signalling course & took up his duties as Brigade Signals Officer: normal day.	
	6-7-17		B/178 shelled from 7 A.M. to 12 p.m. with 180 to 5.9's. The only damage done was 2 spokes broken in gun wheel. Brigade sports held. 5.30 A.M. enemy plane attacked our O.B. at METZ & brought it down in flames.	
	7-7-17		Normal day.	
	8-7-17		Enemy bombarded our front & support line in R.21. & 27. (Right Coy. Right Batn.) in retaliation with concentrations A & B. Enemy Artillery active. 800 rds in all	

Army Form C. 2118

WAR DIARY
or
INTELLIGENCE SUMMARY
(Erase heading not required.)

Instructions regarding War Diaries and Intelligence Summaries are contained in F.S. Regs., Part II. and the Staff Manual respectively. Title Pages will be prepared in manuscript.

Place	Date	Hour	Summary of Events and Information	Remarks and references to Appendices
In the Field.	9.7.17		Our front & support lines again bombarded in R.21 + 27. 900 rds in all. Enemy Arty active	
	10.7.17		Enemy Artillery active on GONNELIEU + our support line.	
	11.7.17		Quieter day. Normal.	
	12.7.17		GONNELIEU shelled with 77mm during the day. E.A. unsuccessfully attacked our O.B. at HEUDICOURT.	
	13.7.17		Normal day. Brigade H.Q. moved from W.10. central to X.7.c.05.60.	
	14.7.17		Enemy Artillery active around R.33.D. Aerial activity normal.	
	15.7.17		Enemy ranged with high air bursts on A/178 position at 11.15 A.M. at 12.30 p.m. the position was shelled with 130 rds 5.9's. No damage done.	
	16.7.17		Quiet day. E.A. unsuccessfully attacked our O.B. at HEUDECOURT. 2nd/Lt BLUNDELL reported for duty & was posted to C/178. B.G.R.A. held conference at these H.Q. with O.C.'s Left, Centre & Right Group.	
	17.7.17		Normal. Capt Powell R.F.A. reported for duty & was posted to B/178. 2nd/Lt. Holmes Sam rejoined B/178.	
	18.7.17		Good sniping day. We fired 87 rounds. No movement seen. 2nd/Lt A Olmshaw appointed adjutant. & Lt Mann posted to D/178.	

WAR DIARY or INTELLIGENCE SUMMARY

Army Form C. 2118

(Erase heading not required.)

Instructions regarding War Diaries and Intelligence Summaries are contained in F.S. Regs., Part II. and the Staff Manual respectively. Title Pages will be prepared in manuscript.

Place	Date	Hour	Summary of Events and Information	Remarks and references to Appendices
	19-7-17		Quiet day. Nothing to report.	
	20-7-17		Normal Artillery activity; 15 E.A. over our lines during day.	
	21-7-17		Heavy hostile artillery fire on 296 Bde Batteries. S.O.S. rocket fired at 10 p.m. O.K. A/178 established their one gun in X.3.	
	22-7-17		Artillery active on both sides.	
	23-7-17		Hostile T.M. at X.12.c.9.1. X.12.c.2.9. & X.18.c.5.5 shooting on Right Brigade front. At request of 296 Bde R.F.A. our D Battery fired 84 rds on T.M. & silenced them. 2nd Lt. Stevens, A/178 wounded at O.P.	
	24-7-17		Capt. Bannister rejoined the unit & was posted to B/178.	
	25-7-17		Enemy registered his own front line R.28.D.2.3 to R.28.D.4.2. & in consequence our Black Watch scheme was cancelled.	
	26-7-17	6 A.M.	Enemy put up heavy barrage on Right Brigade front, & raided our trenches; 25 of our men missing; Hostile artillery from 6 to 7.15 A.M.	
	27-7-17		Normal day.	
	28-7-17		Unusual artillery activity on both sides; One of our 'Planes flew low twice over Gonnelieu & Boche front line & was not fired on.	

War Diary. contd.

Date.		
29-7-17.	Quiet day: observation poor owing to rain.	
30-7-17.	2/Lt Lloyd & Bdr. Ward proceeded to England to attend signalling course at Dunstable. III Corps sports.	
31-7-17.	Normal day. 181 Bde R.F.A sports.	

[signature]
Lt Col: R.F.A.
Commandg. 178th Brigade R.F.A.

WAR DIARY
INTELLIGENCE SUMMARY
(Erase heading not required.)

Army Form C. 2118.

178 Bde. R.F.A.

Place	Date	Hour	Summary of Events and Information	Remarks and references to Appendices
In the field	Aug 1st 1917		Quiet day: night of 1/2 Aug. 12th S.W.B. raided enemy trenches in R.2.2.C. Zero 1 A.M. we bombarded for 1½ hours. No prisoners captured + our troops sustained 18 casualties: a second raid by the right battalion, on the same piece of line 1½ hours afterwards, resulted in 8 casualties to us + one prisoner.	
	" 2nd	AM 10 A.M.	we ceased to be with the Group, + became Right Group. (178 Bde + C/276) A + B/178 also, the gun pits, to shoot on the role of the Group front. The 52nd are to cover 121st + 119 Infantry Brigades for 24 hours.	
	" 3.	AM 10.A.M.	ceased to cover 119, + only cover 121 Inf. Bde. Normal day.	
	" 4.		Nothing to report	
	" 5.		Quiet day: 3 E.A. over our lines in the evening: Col Parsons proceeded on tour of inspection of R.E. Parks at Boulogne and ST OMER. Major Parks in command.	
	" 6.		Much aerial activity during day. Leave resumed.	
	" 7.		Nil.	
	" 8.		Normal day: Col Parsons returned from tour of inspection.	
	" 9.		Nil.	
	" 10.		Major S. Drakes C/178 proceeded to England to be instructor at school of gunnery Shoeburyness.	

Army Form C. 2118.

WAR DIARY
of
INTELLIGENCE SUMMARY.
(Erase heading not required.)

178 Bde R.F.A.

Place	Date	Hour	Summary of Events and Information	Remarks and references to Appendices
	1917 Aug. 11	6	Normal day; Artillery on both sides quiet.	
	" 12th		Unexpected Divisional relief by enemy; we did much night firing on tracks, roads &c.	
	" 13th		During day enemy carried out considerable registration on parts of our line. Also on A/178.	
	" 14th		Very quiet day; considerable aerial activity on both sides in the evening.	
	" 15th		Artillery on both sides quiet; several squadrons of Enemy planes attempted to fly over our line, but were turned back by A.A. fire.	
	" 16th		Normal day; explosion at SONNET FARM men seen to leave hurriedly. 9 section A/178 took 1 section out of action "formed Combi Group 35th DA for purpose of taking part in the capture of "THE KNOLL" & GUILLEMONT FARM.	
	" 17th		A/178 pulled out remainder of Battery.	
	" 18th		Artillery normal; considerable aeroplane activity on both sides.	
	" 19th		Enemy working on his trenches in R 26. Good sniping done by our batteries 35th Div. attacked & captured THE KNOLL & GUILLEMONT FARM.	
	" 20th		1 E.A. brought down by A.A. fire, just South of VILLERS GUISLAIN.	

Army Form C. 2118.

WAR DIARY
INTELLIGENCE SUMMARY
(Erase heading not required.)

178 Bde. R.F.A.

Instructions regarding War Diaries and Intelligence Summaries are contained in F. S. Regs. Part II. and the Staff Manual respectively. Title pages will be prepared in manuscript.

Place	Date 1917	Hour	Summary of Events and Information	Remarks and references to Appendices
	Aug 21st	—	Quiet day: E.A. brought down by A.A. fire in direction BANTEAU. 35th Div. raided enemy's line in OSSUS WOOD. We co-operated by bombarding LES TRANCHEES from 11 p.m. to 11.46 p.m. A/178 returned to Group.	
	" 22		Quiet day: good sniping in R.28. explosions & fire reported in rear of enemy's lines.	
	" 23		Normal day: considerable aeroplane activity. 3rd Bonnyfield hooked to D/178.	
	" 24		Enemy carried out considerable registration of our trenches R.34 & 35. At 7.15 p.m. started a heavy bombardment, which continued until 8.35 p.m. we retaliated with 2 concentrations, & S.O. Lol. Hours into BANTEAU.	
	" 25	4.25 A.M.	Enemy wir raided enemy post (FIFE POST) without result: we fired concentration W¹ in retaliation for attempted enemy raid. D.A. Shorts C/296 pulled out & left the group. Right Group now consists of 178 Bde only. nothing to report.	
	" 26			
	" 27		Quiet day: aerial activity nil.	
	" 28		Nothing to report: weather very wet. 2nd Lt Deardon proceeded to PARIS (Brigade Signals Officer)	

Army Form C. 2118.

178 Bde. R.F.A.

WAR DIARY
INTELLIGENCE SUMMARY.
(Erase heading not required.)

Instructions regarding War Diaries and Intelligence Summaries are contained in F. S. Regs., Part II. and the Staff Manual respectively. Title pages will be prepared in manuscript.

Place	Date	Hour	Summary of Events and Information	Remarks and references to Appendices
	1917. Aug 29		A quiet day: nothing to report.	
	" 30		Enemy artillery fairly active on our trenches in X.7. R.34 & R.35. T.M. seen to shoot from R.29.c.05.60. are retaliated.	
	" 31		At 4:30 A.M. enemy bombarded our front & support line from Turners Quarry to Newton's Post with T.M.'s & 77's. we retaliated. At 4:50 A.M. enemy attacked & captured the Knoll.	

1-9-17.

[signature]
Lt. Col: R.F.A.
Commdg: 178th Brigade R.F.A.

178 Bde R?D
Army Form C. 2118.

WAR DIARY
INTELLIGENCE SUMMARY
(Erase heading not required.)

Instructions regarding War Diaries and Intelligence Summaries are contained in F.S. Regs., Part II. and the Staff Manual respectively. Title pages will be prepared in manuscript.

Place	Date	Hour	Summary of Events and Information	Remarks and references to Appendices
In field	1-9-17		Our batteries did much shooting at movement on F.28; hostile activity; overnight: at 11.35 p.m. enemy bombarded our right battalion front; retaliated with concentration W.	
	2-9-17		Quiet day; our planes active in the evening.	
	3-9-17		Nothing to report; at 9.20 & 11.30 p.m. fired 2 minutes concentration in cooperation with 121 Machine Gun Coy.	
	4-9-17		Normal day.	
	5-9-17		Considerable enemy aerial activity; good shooting by our A.A. + E.A. did not penetrate.	
	6-9-17		About 3.15 p.m. enemy fired 8 rds 5.9's on QUENTIN MILL & GOUZEAUCOURT STATION also a few 4.2's on GAUCHE WOOD.	
	7-9-17		A quiet day. Americans started preparing track for broad-gauge railway by H.Q.	
	8-9-17		Silent raid by 13th Yorks; no result; we fired for 5 minutes to cover their retreat.	
	9-9-17		Nil.	
	10-9-17		Normal day; aeroplanes active.	
	11-9-17		Enemy artillery active; 18 rds 4.2's on VILLERS GUISLAIN + 30 rds 77's on X.5.C.	
	12-9-17		About 40 rds 4.2's on & around ROBERT'S AVENUE.	
	13-9-17		Divisional concentration on BLEAK SUPPORT at 9.45 p.m.	

Army Form C. 2118.

WAR DIARY
or
INTELLIGENCE SUMMARY.
(Erase heading not required.)

Instructions regarding War Diaries and Intelligence Summaries are contained in F. S. Regs., Part II. and the Staff Manual respectively. Title pages will be prepared in manuscript.

Place	Date	Hour	Summary of Events and Information	Remarks and references to Appendices
	14-9-17		Enemy artillery active on GAUCHE WOOD + QUENTIN MILL + R.25. during day. about 80 rounds 4.2's + 77's.	
	15-9-17		GONNELIEU shelled with about 36 rds 5.9's.	
	16-9-17		9 p.m. Left Battalion 35th Div. raided OSSUS WOOD : we fired 6 guns in support of same : 3 prisoners captured.	
	17-9-17		40 rds 4.2's on GOUZEAUCOURT during afternoon : A/178 one man wounded.	
	18-9-17		Nil.	
	19-9-17		Nothing to report.	
	20-9-17		12.20 p.m. Enemy Artillery commenced shelling 6" Hows in VILLERS GUISLAIN : about 250 rds 5.9's & some 4.2's were fired ; ceased shelling at 7 p.m. D/178 moved 2 Hows into BEAUCAMP to assist 181 Bty raid by H.L.I.	
	21-9-17		Our O.B. at HEUDECOURT shelled with H.V. 8" rds.	
	22-9-17		120th Brigade raided FARM TRENCH under smoke screen at 7.10 p.m. 10 prisoners captured. 1st train ran on GOUZAUCOURT to CHAPEL CROSSING to GOUZEAUCOURT.	
	23-9-17		"Q" R.H.A. Battery joined Group, + went into action at X.2.c.90.10.	

Army Form C. 2118.

WAR DIARY
of
INTELLIGENCE SUMMARY.
(Erase heading not required)

Instructions regarding War Diaries and Intelligence Summaries are contained in F. S. Regs., Part II. and the Staff Manual respectively. Title pages will be prepared in manuscript.

Place	Date	Hour	Summary of Events and Information	Remarks and references to Appendices
	24-9-17		Considerable aerial activity; own batteries & hostil carried out registration on R.28. O.B. at HENDECOURT shelled 12 rds. Lt. THORP joined A/178.	
	25-9-17		Artillery on both sides very active: own heavies & field guns carried out registration & cut wire for raid on R.28. Hostile artillery fired throughout the day, 4" H.V. on battery positions (empty) on X.Y. & 5.9's on R.25. (A/181) At 7.30. 12th Suffolks raided R.28. Right Group consisting of 20.6" Hows 2-6"How 6-4.5 Hows & 21 field guns. Barraged for 1 hour & 3 minutes. 10.h.m. "Q" R.H.A. left the group.	
	26-9-17		Normal day: all guns & hows of group moved to rearward positions.	
	27-9-17		B.G.R.A. awarded Military Medal to Gunner Drake D/178. Fired on job in wire R.28.D.	
	28-9-17		Nil during night, fired on job in R.28.D.	
	29-9-17		Nothing to report.	
	30-9-17		Hostile Artillery active on battery positions 181; also 4.2's on VILLERS GUISLAIN. Own batteries fired 90 rds during night on R.28.D & R.29.C.	

K J Barrow
Lt. Col.: R.F.A.
Commdg: 178th Brigade R.F.A.

Secret.

17th Bn A.F.A Army Form C. 2118.

WAR DIARY
or
INTELLIGENCE SUMMARY.
(Erase heading not required.)

Instructions regarding War Diaries and Intelligence Summaries are contained in F.S. Regs., Part II. and the Staff Manual respectively. Title pages will be prepared in manuscript.

Place	Date	Hour	Summary of Events and Information	Remarks and references to Appendices
In the field	Oct 1st 1917		Enemy shelling above normal, chiefly around X.5, -7 & 8. Roberts Avenue. Our Artillery fired 110 rds. on R.28.D. + R.29 a. during night. D/78 moved forward to Villers Guislain.	
	- 2nd		Normal day: nothing to report.	
	- 3rd		Hostile Artillery active on right Battalion front.	
	- 4th		Quiet day: C/178 fired 20 rds Thermit shell as test: Infantry informed & reported unsuccessful.	
	- 5th		8.40 p.m. 119 Infantry Brigade raided enemy trenches at R.15. many of the enemy killed no prisoners: we fired in assistance. Enemy Artillery exceptionally active throughout the day on X.7 and Chapel Crossing. D/178 had 1 O.R. wounded by shell at Villers Guislain. 1 man about 400 rds. fired killed & 2 wounded. 5.26 A.M. enemy bombarded left Battalion front with 4.7's + T.M's. We fired 2 concentrations & counter preparation: all fired at 6.21 A.M. Capt Dimble 14th A + S.H. attached to Brigade, enlarging staff – counts were 9.30 p.m. our Artillery fired concentration on Bleak Support.	
	6th		Quiet day	
	7th		Nothing to report.	
	8th		Hostile Artillery active R.31 & X.1. about 300 rds fired. disturbed enemy divisional relief.	

Army Form C. 2118.

WAR DIARY
of
INTELLIGENCE SUMMARY.
(Erase heading not required.)

178 Brigade R.F.A.

Instructions regarding War Diaries and Intelligence Summaries are contained in F. S. Regs. Part II. and the Staff Manual respectively. Title pages will be prepared in manuscript.

Place	Date 1917	Hour	Summary of Events and Information	Remarks and references to Appendices
In the field	Oct 9		Quiet day. 119 Infantry Brigade relieved by 118 Brigade 20th Division. Lt. Col. W.F. Parsons D.S.O. R.F.A. proceeded on leave to England.	
	- 10		Hostile Artillery active around GOUZEAUCOURT WOOD. 20.106.77½ on B/178.	
	- 11		Nothing to report.	
	- 12		Observation conditions bad. Quiet day.	
	- 13		Hostile Artillery active around R.3.K.B.	
	- 14		G.O.C. R.A. inspected Brigade wagon lines. Normal.	
	- 15		Hostile Artillery active. GONNELIEU - R.184 - + VILLERS GUISLAIN shelled. Lt Col. Duke 72 A. & S.H. finished period of attachment.	
	- 16		20th Divisional Commander inspected our front + O.Pis. 121 Battery shelled R.S.M. GILKES left Brigade. A/R.S.M. ROUSE posted.	
	- 17		Hostile shelling on our front + support lines. Much aerial activity.	
	- 18		Hostile shelling, about 300.10b. on X.7. (Ammunition R.F.A.) Major R. RASHLEIGH D.S.O. M.C. R.F.A. rejoined Brigade + posted to A/178.	
	- 19		Nil.	

Army Form C. 2118.

WAR DIARY
INTELLIGENCE SUMMARY.
(Erase heading not required.)

Instructions regarding War Diaries and Intelligence Summaries are contained in F. S. Regs., Part II. and the Staff Manual respectively. Title pages will be prepared in manuscript.

Place	Date 1917	Hour	Summary of Events and Information	Remarks and references to Appendices
In field	Oct 20		GONNELIEU shelled: aircraft activity	
	-21		Considerable activity on both sides, on the air. Quiet day.	
	-22		Normal: one pulled half our guns out the line + 20th D.A. took equal number of guns into action. Col. Parsons returned from leave.	
	-23		Nothing to report: normal day.	
	-24		Relief by 91st Brigade R.F.A. 20th D.A. complete.	
	-25		Brigade billeted at wagon lines.	
	-26		Nil.	
	-27		A/175 + H.Q. entrained for ESQUELBECQ; R/M R.T.O. PERONNE received orders to carry rest of D.A. Brigade on march at ST DENIS.	
	-28		Nil.	
	-29		Nil.	
	-30		B/175 Ad. shill order.	
	-31		Nil.	

Ar7091. Wt. W18839/M1298. 750,000. 1/17. D.D & L., Ltd. Forms/C2118/12.

H. Henshaw Capt. R.F.A.
Adjutant 175 A Brigade R.F.A.
for Lt. Col. Comdg.

SECRET.
                                                59th Div. Artillery.
                                                No. S/609/G.
                                                26/2/18.

Centre Group.
Left Group.
59th D.F.H.Q.
40th D.T.M.O.
59th Division "G"
VIth Corps R.A.
177th Inf. Bde.
178th Inf. Bde.

    An Artillery concentration on the FACTORY in U.23.a & b. will take place at 5.30 p.m. February 27th.

    The following will take part :-

2 4.5" Hows. - Centre Group.
2 4.5" Hows. - Left Group.
3 6" Newton T.Ms - X/59 T.M. Battery

One Section of 18-prs Centre Group will fire on POM ALLEY with AX.

Rates of Fire 18-prs & 4.5" Hows - 3 rounds per gun per minute.

            Trench Mortars - 3 rounds per min.

    Firing will cease at 5.40 p.m.

    Watches will be synchronised from this Office at 3.30 p.m.

    ACKNOWLEDGE.

                                              Captain, R.A.,
26/10/17.   Brigade Major, R.A., 59th Division.

WAR DIARY or INTELLIGENCE SUMMARY

Army Form C. 2118

178 Brigade R.F.A. 40 Div^n   Vol 18

Place	Date	Hour	Summary of Events and Information	Remarks and references to Appendices
1917 In the field	Nov. 1st		Brigade moved into camp at NURLU. B/178 calibrated 4 guns at PERONNE range.	
	2nd		C/178 calibrated 5 guns at PERONNE. Brigade working on fatigues.	
	3			
	4			
	5		Whole of brigade and 4 officers 95 men of the 2nd + 21st Brigade, 6th Division attached to us, worked on fatigues, making gun pits, carrying ammunition + rubble for roads.	
	6			
	7			
	8		A/178 calibrated 4 guns. B/178 2 guns	
	9		D/178 5 75mm.	
	10		Still on fatigues + in camp at NURLU	
	11			
	12		NURLU.	
	13		Brigade moved to EQUANCOURT.	
	14		Guns taken into action in front of GOUZEAUCOURT (R.20) and 2 men per battery left with the guns, detachments returned to EQUANCOURT. Major R.N. WALLIS went into hospital with gastritis.	
	15		All officers recalled from leave. A/178 drew 2 guns from I.O.M. EQUANCOURT.	
	16		A/178 calibrated their 2 new guns + D/178 on road.	
	17		Normal days.	
	18			

Army Form C. 2118

WAR DIARY
INTELLIGENCE SUMMARY
(Erase heading not required.)

178 Brigade R.F.A. 40th Divn.

Place	Date 1917	Hour	Summary of Events and Information	Remarks and references to Appendices
In the field	Nov.19		"Y" day for the battle. Brigade went into action front of GONZEAUCOURT with H.Q. at TR25. (Sheet 57c.SE)	
	-20		Zero day: 6.20.A.M. Zero hour. 6th Division on left. 20th Division in centre and 12th Division on our right. 178 Bde in left Group, commanded by Col. Erskine 9th Bde R.F.A. 20th Divn. No preliminary bombardment; at Zero -10, Infantry assisted by large numbers small & large tanks moved forward to attack. Zero hour, artillery barrage opened & went on to 9.55 A.M. Complete surprise to enemy; numbers of prisoners captured, & our troops advanced (cavalry & infantry) to MARCOING, RIBECOURT, & the 62nd Division through HAVRINCOURT.	
		A.10.A.M.	178 Bde pulled out of action & went back to billets in EQUANCOURT.	
		2 p.m.	Brigade marched into HAPLINCOURT & stayed for the night.	
	-21	11 A.M.	Lt. Col. Comdg. summoned to G.O.C. 40th D.A. & received instructions to move into action South of GRAINCOURT; Colonel went forward to reconnoitre, B.C.'s followed, & the Brigade moved from HAPLINCOURT at 2.20 p.m.	
	-22		Left Group, with H.Q. in catacombs GRAINCOURT, consisting of 310 Bde R.F.A. (Lt.Col. D. Antrobus) 312 Bde R.F.A. (Major Eaton) (both 62nd Div. Arty) and 178 Bde Group commanded by Lt.Col.N.F. Parsons D.S.O. R.F.A.	

WAR DIARY
or
INTELLIGENCE SUMMARY
(Erase heading not required.)

Army Form C. 2118

Place	Date 1917	Hour	Summary of Events and Information	Remarks and references to Appendices
In the field	Nov 23	at 10.30 A.M.	(Zero hour) with 36th Division on our left, 40th Division in centre and 51st Division on right, our troops, assisted by tanks, attacked BOURLON village and Wood; and FONTAINE. 36th Division made no progress, our Division got through the village but owing to heavy machine gun fire could not hold on; 51st made no progress on right.	
	— 24th		Reinforcements, consisting of 1 cavalry Brigade brought up; again attacked BOURLON village & wood, but could not hold on, having no support from their left.	
	— 25th		62nd Division relieved 40th Division. 187 Bde relieved 121, 8 A.m. 121 of 40th by left group; 186 Bde (Brig Gen Bradford V.C.) relieved 119 & covered by right group. (Brig Gen Taylor) & covered	
	— 26.		Right & Left Group Bty H.Q. 186 & 187 Bdes H.Q. (Inf) moved from GRAINCOURT to K.11.A.2.7. (8 A.m. 4.2 position)	
	— 27.		62nd Division again attacked Bourlon village & wood, with Guards Division on our right, and 2nd Division on left, assisted by artillery & tanks. Zero hour 6.20 A.M. our barrage continued until 10.5 A.M. after which we fired heavy & continual bursts of fire on the enemy. Guards Div made no progress, & our line remained the same after the battle.	

Army Form C. 2118

WAR DIARY
INTELLIGENCE SUMMARY
(Erase heading not required.)

178 Brigade R.F.A. 40th Divn.

Place	Date	Hour	Summary of Events and Information	Remarks and references to Appendices
In the field	Nov. 28		Hostile Artillery active around Sugar Factory & GRAINCOURT.	
"	29		47th Division (less artillery) relieved the 62nd Division in the line. 140 Bde relieving 187 & covered by left Group. 141 Bde relieved the 186 Bde & covered by right Group. (Groups under 62" D.A.)	
"	30	8.40 A.M.	enemy put down heavy Artillery barrage, also smoke barrage on left of BOURLON Wood, under cover of which he heavily attacked our positions on 2nd 47th & Guards Divisional fronts. Our Batteries opened on their S.O.S. barrage at 8.46.	
		At 11.20	enemy seen advancing in strength over the ridge in E.16. The whole of the Group switched to the left & fired over open sights, rapid, for 15 minutes, when enemy were seen to retire, disorganised.	
		12.55.	Group stopped firing. During afternoon, 2.45 p.m. S.O.S. seen to go up from Sugar Factory, opened on S.O.S. barrage line at 2.47 p.m. about 5 p.m. situation cleared, & we stopped firing. Capt Reid D/178. and 2nd 2 Sergts wounded.	

In the field.

Stonehouse Capt & adj.
for Lt Col Comdg 178 Bde R.F.A.

Army Form C. 2118.

WAR DIARY
or
INTELLIGENCE SUMMARY.

(Erase heading not required.)

178 Bde R.F.A.

178 Bde R.F.A.

Place	Date	Hour	Summary of Events and Information	Remarks and references to Appendices
In the field	1.12.17		Hostile artillery active on GRAINCOURT & the SUGAR FACTORY. Enemy attacked in force on our left; we fired S.O.S. from 3pm to 4.5pm no attack was made on our front. 7.30pm fired S.O.S. until 7.38pm nothing developed. Considerable aerial activity; 2nd Lt Payne 6/16. shot down E.A with a Lewis gun from battery position. 2 officers of the Brigade wounded	
	2.12.17		Our batteries still in the open, & in direct observation from the enemy; were shelled & suffered casualties. 12.47. 2 enemy field seen to be brought into action on crest in E.18. (N. of Bourlon Wood) engaged & crew seen to leave gun; one gun certainly smashed & other one damaged. Casualties inflicted on enemy. 8.10pm. 140 Infy. Bde under barrage by Left Group & assisted by groups on either side, advanced their line. 4.00 yds. 2 enemy officers & 54 O.R. 16 M.G. captured, satisfactory results. Usual harassing fire carried out during night by group.	
	3.12.17		Under orders from group commander, 2 batteries moved their position, owing to being in direct observation of enemy. 1pm. 97 D.A report that our troops seen forced on E.18.0.1.9 but are apparently an isolated party & will be recalled at night.	

WAR DIARY
INTELLIGENCE SUMMARY.
(Erase heading not required.)

Army Form C. 2118.

Place	Date	Hour	Summary of Events and Information	Remarks and references to Appendices
In the field	3/12/17		142 Inf Bde relieved the 140 Bde	
		10.25 a.m.	enemy put down heavy barrage on East edge of Bourlon Wood	
			Opened S.O.S. immediately: ceased firing at 11.8 a.m. as no hostile action followed. Capt Foss wounded.	
			Right Group (Lt Col Palmer) 3 Brigade, pulled out of action to wagon lines	
			Left Group covered whole of Divisional front. Usual night firing	
	4/12/17		Group H.Q. shelled. 2.20 p.m. enemy reported massing in E.17.	
		2.26 p.m.	S.O.S. fired till 2.49 p.m. no hostile action developed.	
			Retirement from Bourlon salient ordered: outpost line formed by 140 Inf Bde.	
			Left Group instructed batteries from action between 6 p.m. & 9.30 p.m. & went into action in HAVRINCOURT K.27. 28. 29. 22.	
			Group H.Q. at K.27.D.4.1. Group covers 142 Inf Bde with 3 Batts.	
			140 Inf Bde with 1 Battn in the line	
			All hostile guns captured by us were destroyed prior to evacuation. dug-outs blown up & ammunition retrieved	
			Withdrawal carried out to programme.	

Army Form C. 2118.

WAR DIARY
or
INTELLIGENCE SUMMARY.
(Erase heading not required.)

Instructions regarding War Diaries and Intelligence Summaries are contained in F. S. Regs., Part II. and the Staff Manual respectively. Title pages will be prepared in manuscript.

Place	Date	Hour	Summary of Events and Information	Remarks and references to Appendices
In the field	5.12.17		Carried out observed shooting on enemy seen continually advancing. 3 p.m. enemy occupied ANNEUX and the SUGAR FACTORY. Bde. wagon lines moved to MONTMARTRE Q.S.D. 47 D.A. H.Q. moved to K.32.D.8.4. Harassing fire continued during night.	
	6.12.17		Outpost line retired to main Defensive Positions ; Left Group now covering 148 Bde. + 2 Battalions 190 Bde. Fired considerable amount during day on enemy from O.P.'s. Enemy line reported to run K.5.g.5.3 — K.6.c.8.0. Our field guns + howrs. shelled GRAINCOURT. Usual night firing carried out.	
	7.12.17		HAVRINCOURT shelled + bombed. Group carried out considerable sniping + inflicted casualties on enemy. Group H.Q. shelled. 1 man killed, 2 wounded. 47 D.A. H.Q. moved to YTRES.	
	8.12.17		6.30 A.M. opened on S.O.S. at request of Infantry ; no action by enemy followed. Stopped firing 6.47 A.M. Group H.Q. moved to dugout in trench at K.32.D.2.4. 7 p.m. Right Group (Lt Col Palmer 181) covered 2 Battalions 190 O Bde +	

Army Form C. 2118.

WAR DIARY
or
INTELLIGENCE SUMMARY.
(Erase heading not required.)

Instructions regarding War Diaries and Intelligence Summaries are contained in F. S. Regs., Part II. and the Staff Manual respectively. Title pages will be prepared in manuscript.

Place	Date	Hour	Summary of Events and Information	Remarks and references to Appendices
3rd In the field	8/12/17	contd.	Left Group covered 3 battalions 142 Bde. Usual night firing carried out, in addition 400 gas shell were fired into GRAINCOURT by group.	
	9/12/17	8.20 am.	our O.P. reported S.O.S rockets on our front: fired S.O.S from 8.25 to 9.10 pm. Enemy rushed & captured one of our forward posts at K.4.D.1.5. Group fired in reply to request of infantry, several times during day.	
		3.30 pm	S.O.S. reported by our O.P. fired S.O.S until 3.46 pm.	
		5.7 pm	S.O.S. from infantry: fired S.O.S. till 6 pm. Group this day fired over 9000 rds in reply to requests from infantry. No serious enterprise attempted by enemy. 200 rds per battery night firing. Bde. wagon lines shelled & bombed.	
	10/12/17		Hostile artillery active around HAVRINCOURT. considerable aerial activity on both sides. Usual 200 rds per battery night firing.	

Army Form C. 2118.

WAR DIARY
INTELLIGENCE SUMMARY.
(Erase heading not required.)

Instructions regarding War Diaries and Intelligence Summaries are contained in F. S. Regs., Part II. and the Staff Manual respectively. Title pages will be prepared in manuscript.

Place	Date	Hour	Summary of Events and Information	Remarks and references to Appendices
In the field	11/12/17	3.10 pm	S.O.S. fired until 3.26 pm - no hostile action	
			181 Bde relieved out the line, & 77th Army Bde covered sheet front	
		12 noon	191 Inf Bde relieved the 140 Bde. (1 Batt.)	
			Col. Bowring O.C. 236 Bde R.F.A. 47th Divn arrived at group H.Q. to take over	
		6 pm	178 Bde relieved by pulled out of the line & went to wagon lines	
		3.10 & 3.12	Bde Brigade covered the group front	
	12/12/17	8 A.M.	77th Army Bde came under Left Group, whch covered the whole of Divisional front (4 Batt. in line)	
		10 A.M	Command of Left group passed to Col. Bowring R.F.A.	
			Group H.Q. pulled out to wagon lines, & took the road to HAMELINCOURT.	
			Batteries of 178 marched at 8.30 A.M. to HAMELINCOURT & on arrival went into action under Lt. Col. David R.F.A. 180 Bde - 16th Divs in & around ST LEGER area: VI Corps	
			Bde H.Q. arrived at wagon lines in S.17.A (N of HAMELINCOURT)	
	13.12.17		Bde H.Q. 178 Bde do not command the group, remained at Wagon lines	

WAR DIARY or INTELLIGENCE SUMMARY

Army Form C. 2118.

Place	Date	Hour	Summary of Events and Information	Remarks and references to Appendices
14.12.17	14.12.17		H.Q. at wagon lines	
	15.12.17		- do -	
	16.12.17		- do -	
	17.12.17		Lt. Col. Conly attended conference at D.A. H.Q.	
	18.12.17		Nil.	
	19.12.17		Regiment went forward to left Group H.Q. & commenced taking over. Also regimt. officers. Lt. Col. Parsons DSO RFA proceeded to England on course of instruction.	
	20.12.17		178 Bde commanded by Major D.L. Dutton took command of Left Group (consisting of 178 Bde + 65th & O.Bty A/14 Battery of 14 A.F.A.) with H.Q. at ST LEGER T.28.B.10.90. from Lt Col Daud.	
	21.12.17		Situation normal. Nothing to report.	
	22nd		Normal period. We carried out night & day shoots took artillery fired a few rounds on CROISELLES & ST LEGER, otherwise quiet. Weather very misty. aerial activity Nil.	
	23rd			
	24th			
	25th			
	26th			
	27th			

Army Form C. 2118.

WAR DIARY
or
INTELLIGENCE SUMMARY.
(Erase heading not required.)

Instructions regarding War Diaries and Intelligence Summaries are contained in F. S. Regs., Part II. and the Staff Manual respectively. Title pages will be prepared in manuscript.

Place	Date	Hour	Summary of Events and Information	Remarks and references to Appendices
In the field	28/12/17		At 10 AM. became Right Group 34th D.A. no change in batteries & cover the same front; now held by 101 Inf Bde 34th Div who relieved the 120 Inf Bde 40th Div.	
	29.12.17		Increase in aerial activity	
	30.12.17		Period quite normal.	
	31.12.17			

J Stonehewer Capt + adj

Col: R.F.A.
for
Comndg: 178th Brigade R.F.A.

Army Form C. 2118.

WAR DIARY
or
INTELLIGENCE SUMMARY.
(Erase heading not required.)

178 Bde. R.F.A.

Instructions regarding War Diaries and Intelligence Summaries are contained in F. S. Regs., Part II. and the Staff Manual respectively. Title pages will be prepared in manuscript.

Place	Date	Hour	Summary of Events and Information	Remarks and references to Appendices
In field	January 1918			
	" 1st		Nothing special to report. B/178 moved 4 guns to new position, much aerial activity. A/14 moved 2 guns in forward section Moeuvres	
	" 2nd		Normal activity both sides.	
	" 3rd		D/178 moved one section forward. Hostile artillery active around CROISILLES; about 300 rds phosgene & 4.2"s were fired. 2. E.A. ours. Capt Macintosh of 16th Royal Scots. (35 Divn) attached for 48 hours to A/14.	
	" 4th		Clear day; considerable aerial activity both sides; normal day.	
	" 5th		Nil.	
	" 6th		A/14 pulled out of action & went to wagon lines. Hostile activity below normal.	
	" 7th		68th O.By R.F.A pulled out of action; group now consists of 178 Bde. R.F.A. less 1 section D/178 attached to left group. 40th D.A.	
	" 8th " 9th " 10th		Usual day & night harassing fire carried out, nothing to report.	

Army Form C. 2118.

WAR DIARY
INTELLIGENCE SUMMARY.
(Erase heading not required.)

Instructions regarding War Diaries and Intelligence Summaries are contained in F. S. Regs., Part II. and the Staff Manual respectively. Title pages will be prepared in manuscript. No. 2. 178 Bde R.F.A

Place	Date	Hour	Summary of Events and Information	Remarks and references to Appendices
In the field	January 1918			
	11th		Lt Coles of 34th Divn (infantry) attached for 48 hours to D/178.	
	12th		Detached section D/178 returned, after being attached to left group & O.D.A Normal day.	
	13th		Hostile activity normal. Quiet day. A/178 moved one section.	
	14.		Nothing to report. 26 men exchanged with D.A.C. for training.	
	15th		Usual day & night firing ; hostile artillerie normal.	
	16th		Nil.	
	17th		Nothing to report.	
	18th		B/178 one section shelled ; 1 gun slightly damaged. considerable aerial activity.	
	19th } 20.		Normal days.	

Army Form C. 2118.

WAR DIARY
or
INTELLIGENCE SUMMARY.
(Erase heading not required.)

Instructions regarding War Diaries and Intelligence Summaries are contained in F. S. Regs., Part II. and the Staff Manual respectively. Title pages will be prepared in manuscript.

Place	Date	Hour	Summary of Events and Information	Remarks and references to Appendices
In the field	January 1918			
	21		Lt. Col. W.F. Parsons D.S.O. returned from leave. Hostile attitude normal.	
	22		Quiet day.	
	23		Nil.	
	24		F.G.C.M. held re Saddle Bancroft B/178 & G. Freeman D/178. Lewis section C/178 shelled; gun slightly damaged. Lewis section C/178 moved into alt 66° Bty position. Enemy artillery rather more active than usual along group front.	
	25		Hostile artillery active (4.2"s & T.M's) on right battalion front. during night Enemy raided one of our advanced posts & captured 2 men (right battalion front). Left battalion captured 2 Huns in a patrol encounter.	
	26		Normal day; aerial activity Nil.	
	27		Nothing to report.	

Army Form C. 2118.

WAR DIARY
of
INTELLIGENCE SUMMARY.
(Erase heading not required.)

178 Bde. R.F.A.

HQ., 178th BRIGADE, R.F.A.
No. ....
Date ....

Place	Date	Hour	Summary of Events and Information	Remarks and references to Appendices
Trinifeld	January 1918			
	-28		D/178 registered 2 enemy T.M. by aeroplane. Lt. Col. Emely left for 14 days leave with R.F.C. at BERTANGLES. 101 Infantry Brigade 34th Division, relieved by 8th Infantry Bde. 3rd Division. 7.30 p.m. during the night, enemy E.Aeroplane bombed back areas dropping about 200 bombs.	
	-29		Hostile activity normal. 34th D.A. relieved the 34th D.A. considerable aerial activity on both sides. Major F.W. Cook M.C. R.F.A. took over command of the Group vice Major A.L. Wilkes M.C. R.F.A. Enemy again bombed back areas at night.	
	-30		Normal: aerial activity on both sides considerable.	
	-31		Quiet day: Major H.B. Banister R.F.A. took over command of Brigade on his return from leave.	

A. Strickmore Capt & adj
for major comdg 178 Bde R.F.A.

Army Form C. 2118.

WAR DIARY
or
INTELLIGENCE SUMMARY.
(Erase heading not required.)

178 Brigade R.F.A

Place	Date	Hour	Summary of Events and Information	Remarks and references to Appendices
Field	FEBRUARY 1st		Quiet day: considerable aerial activity. 2nd Lt. AULTPORT U.S.A. R.F.A. attached to Group for instruction.	
	2nd		Group carried out usual day & night firing programmes. Nothing to report.	
	3rd		Lt. Col. W.J. PARSONS D.S.O. R.F.A. returned from course with R.F.C. and assumed command 90th D.A.	
	4th		Nil. C.R.A. 3rd D.A. visited Group & Batteries.	
	5th		Normal day: usual harassing fire by group.	
	6th		Nil. very clear day & batteries registered many targets.	
	7th		Nothing unusual to report: 2nd Lt AULTPORT of U.S.A. artillery returned to his unit.	
	8th		6.30 A.M. S.O.S. by night & earlier confirmed of right battalion: enemy attempted to raid one of our forward posts but failed Group fired S.O.S. until 7.30 A.M.	

Army Form C. 2118.

WAR DIARY
or
INTELLIGENCE SUMMARY.
(Erase heading not required.)

178 Brigade R.F.A.

Instructions regarding War Diaries and Intelligence Summaries are contained in F. S. Regs., Part II. and the Staff Manual respectively. Title pages will be prepared in manuscript.

Place	Date	Hour	Summary of Events and Information	Remarks and references to Appendices
Field.	FEBRUARY			
	9"		Hostile Artillery more active than usual, about 150 rds 5.9's from REMY WOOD around B/178 forward section. D/178 carried out counter battery shoot by aid of aeroplane.	
	10"		Much enemy movement in back areas reported.	
	11"		Hostile field guns and T.M's active on our front & support trenches. Much movement in enemy back areas.	
	12"		Nil	
	13"		Hostile movement and activity normal. Lt. Col. W. F. Parsons D.S.O. R.F.A. assumed command of Group.	
	14"		B/178 forward section again shelled by 4.2's. Normal day.	
	15"		Nil.	
	16"		Nil.	

Army Form C. 2118.

WAR DIARY
or
INTELLIGENCE SUMMARY.
(Erase heading not required.)

178 Brigade R.F.A.

Instructions regarding War Diaries and Intelligence Summaries are contained in F. S. Regs., Part II. and the Staff Manual respectively. Title pages will be prepared in manuscript.

Place	Date	Hour	Summary of Events and Information	Remarks and references to Appendices
Field	FEBRUARY 17		Considerable aerial activity on both sides: enemy movement above normal.	
	18		Hostile activity normal: enemy Aeroplanes bombed back areas at night	
	19		Nil. Back areas again bombed by E.A.	
	20		Quiet day. D/178. carried out Gas shell bombardment in conjunction with Heavy Artillery, on enemy Batteries U.B.21. U.B.38. U.B.40. Fired 460 rds B.E.B.R. from 6.30 p.m. to 9.30 p.m.	
	21		A few 4" H.V. (hostile) into BOIRY BECQUERELLE. Normal day.	
	22		Nil. About 11.30 p.m. about 9 rds Gas shell on D/178.	
	23		Activity both aerial & Artillery, Normal.	
	24		About 16 rounds 4.2.8. on HENIN - ST LEGER RD about T.22. at 10 A.M.	

WAR DIARY
or
INTELLIGENCE SUMMARY.
(Erase heading not required.)

Army Form C. 2118.

Instructions regarding War Diaries and Intelligence Summaries are contained in F. S. Regs., Part II. and the Staff Manual respectively. Title pages will be prepared in manuscript. 178 Brigade R.F.A

Place	Date	Hour	Summary of Events and Information	Remarks and references to Appendices
Field	FEBRUARY 25"		About 12 rds 4.2's in vicinity of Group H.Q. Enemy artillery generally more active than usual. 9.33 p.m. S.O.S. from right & centre battalions companies of right battalion. Group fired S.O.S. until 10.6 p.m. Enemy attempted a raid on one of our forward posts, but failed.	
	26"		Normal. 1 E.A. brought down by A.A. fire & fell in our lines.	
	27"		Quiet day. Visit by G.O.C commanding British Armies	
	28"		Enemy artillery + T.M.'s active on our support lines. B/178 forward section shelled by 8 inch.	

Stonehouse Capt. R.F.A.
Adjutant 178th Brigade R.F.A.
for Lt. Col. Comdg.

S E C R E T.   40th. D.A. No. 356/B.M.

Right Group,
Centre Group,
Left Group,
120th. Infantry Brigade,
121st. Infantry Brigade.
40th. Division.
R.A. VI Corps.
----

1.   On the first suitable day when visibility is good an observed destructive shoot will be carried out on BUNNY HUG - as under.

2.   Forward Section D/181 - U.23.c.70.07.)
                              to   ) 100 rounds.
                          U.29.b.60.95.)
                              and
                          U.29.a.70.70.)
                              to   ) 100 rounds.
                          U.29.b.55.65.)

      Forward Section D/295 - U.29.a.70.70.)
                              to   ) 100 rounds.
                          U.23.c.70.07.)
                              &
                          U.29.b.30.70.)
                              to   ) 100 rounds.
                          U.23.d.25.10.)

3.   Groups concerned will arrange time, date, and details, and will notify this Office and Infantry Brigades in time for any necessary arrangements for withdrawal of posts to be made.

9.2.18.   A/Brigade Major, 40th. Divisional Arty.
                                       Captain. R.A.

SECRET.

59th Div. Arty.
No. S/554/G.
15/2/18.

Right Group.   176th Inf. Bde.
Centre Group.   177th   "   "
Left Group.   178th   "   "
D.T.M.O., 59th Div. 54th H.A.G.
59th Div. "G"   R.A. VIth Corps.
                    H.A. VIth

The following Divisional Artillery Concentration will take place from 11.30 a.m. to 11.50 a.m. on February 16th.

Only "active" guns and Hows. will be used.

Right Group	2 4.5" Hows.) 2 18-prs.)	U.22.b.75.50 to U.23.a.20.25
Centre Group	2 4.5" Hows.) 2 18-prs.)	U.22.b.55.30 to U.22.b.75.50
Left Group	2 4.5" Hows.) 2 18-prs.)	U.22.b.55.20 to U.23.a.00.15
54th H.A.G.	2 6" Hows.	U.22.b.55.30 to U.23.a.20.25
	2 6" Hows.	Coy. H.Q. & Trench Junction U.22.b.85.45 Trench and road U.22.b.60.40 to U.22.b.75.50

Rate of Fire.

18-prs -   11.30 am to 11.40 am, 3 rds per gun per min.
            11.40 am to 11.50 am, 2 rds per gun per min.

4.5" Hows.- 11.30 am to 11.50 am, 2 rds per gun per min.

Ammunition.

    18-prs. AX.   4.5" Hows. BX.

Watches will be synchronised from this Office at 10 a.m.

ACKNOWLEDGE.

16th Feb. 1918.

Captain, R.A.,
Brigade Major, R.A., 59th Division.

SECRET.

59th Div. Arty.
No. S/578/G.
20/2/18.

Right Group.
Centre Group.
Left Group.
54th Brigade R.G.A.
46th D.T.M.O.
59th D.T.M.O.
59th Div. "G"
R.A. VIth Corps.
178th Infantry Bde.

The following Artillery Concentration will take place from 10.10 p.m. to 10.25 p.m. on February, 22nd :-

2 6" How. 54th Bde R.G.A.   Dug-outs in Road U.15.c.30.95
                                                to U.15.c.30.70

2 6" Hows. 54th Bde R.G.A.   New work round U.15.c.75.75

2 4.5" Hows.) Left Group   CRUMP ALLEY.
2 18-prs.   )

2 4.5" Hows   Centre Group. (Trench U.15.c.70.95 to
2 18-prs   Left Group.   (U.15.c.80.65.

X.40 T.M.Battery.   Road U.15.c.30.95 to
                                    U.15.c.80.70

Rates of fire:-

18-prs   -   1st 5 minutes, 2 rds per gun per min.
               then onwards, 1 rd per gun per min.

4.5" Hows -   1 round per gun per min.

18-prs will fire AX.   4.5" Hows. DX.

Watches will be synchronised from this Office at 9.15 p.m.   9.40 p.m.

ACKNOWLEDGE.

Captain, R.A.,
20/2/18.   Brigade Major, R.A., 59th Division.

HOWS

```
                                           59th Div. Arty.
                                           No. S/604/G.
54th Bde R.G.A.                            24/2/18.
Right Group.
Centre Group.
Left Group.
59th Div. "G"
R.A., VIth Corps.
176th Infantry Brigade.
177th Infantry Brigade.
178th Infantry Brigade.
```

[stamp: 181st BRIGADE ROYAL FIELD ARTILLERY 25 FEB 1918] 7.876

The following Artillery Concentration will take place on February 25th :-   on Feby 26th

4 3"Hows.	54th Bde R.G.A.	Area.	U.10.d.60.40 - 40.40 - 40.60 - 60.60.
4 18-prs 2 4.5"Hows	Centre Group	Area	U.10.d.80.35 - 60.40 - 75.60 - 90.45.
4 18-prs 2 4.5"Hows.	Left Group.	Area	U.10.d.60.40 - 45.45 - 70.70 - 75.60.

B/181
C/181
D/181

Ammunition.   18-prs AK.   4.5" Hows. EK.

Rates of Fire.	18-prs Rds. per gun per min.	4.5"How. Rds per gun per min
5 p.m. to 5.5 pm	3	2
5.5 pm to 5.10 pm	1	1
5.10 pm to 5.25 pm	STOP	STOP
5.25 pm to 5.30 pm	3	2
5.30 pm	CEASE FIRING.	

Watches will be synchronised from this Office at 3.30 p.m.

ACKNOWLEDGE. ✓

4.0 pm

                                    Captain, R.A.,
24/2/18.   Brigade Major, R.A., 59th Division.

SECRET.

LEFT GROUP 59th D.A.

NIGHT FIRING.

22/23rd Feby.

Period.	Zone "A".		Zone "B".		Zone "C".	
6.00.p.m.to 7.30.p.m.	A/181..	B22 LMS U.21.b.70.70. to U.16.c.35.25. Ammunition:- 75 rds AX.	H.T.M.B.		D/181..	Trench U.10.d.00.65. - Cemetery U.10.d. Ammunition:- 25 rds.H.
7.30.p.m.to 9.30.p.m.		Infantry Patrols.		Machine guns.	C/181..	U.S.P.6. U.S.P.10. Ammunition:- 50 rds.AX.
10.45.p.m to Dawn.		Infantry Patrols.	B/231...	New work in U.15.a.55.29. to U.15.a.47.22. Ammunition:- 75 rds.AX.		

21.2.18..

(signed) Shanks

Lieut.R.F.A.
A/Adjutant,Left Group,59th D.A.

SECRET.

LEFT GROUP 59th D.A.

NIGHT FIRING.

23/24th Feb.

Period.	ZONE A.	ZONE B.	ZONE C.
Dusk to 10.00 p.m.	Infantry Patrols.	Machine Guns. B/181. V.A.P.10. 50 rds.	C/181. FONTAINE-HERMICOURT Road in U.10.c & d. Ammunition. 50 rounds.
10.00 p.m. to midnight.	A/181. TRIDENT ALLEY & DOG TRENCH. Ammunition. 25 rounds. C/181. DOG LANE. Ammunition. 25 rounds.	A/181. UAP.7. & Sunken Rds. in U.15.a. Ammunition. 50 rounds.	
12 midnight to dawn.	Infantry Patrols.	Machine Guns.	D/181. Roads & Tracks in HERMICOURT. Ammunition. 25 Rx.

22.2.18.

Lieut.R.F.A.
A/Adjutant, Left Group,59th D.A.

SECRET.

LEFT GROUP 59th D.A.
===================

NIGHT FIRING.
24/25th Feb.

Period.	ZONE A.	ZONE B.	ZONE C.
Dusk to 2.0.a.m.	Infantry Patrols.	Machine Guns. D/181. COPSE TRENCH in U.16.c. Ammunition:- 75 rounds.	D/181. HENDECOURT CEMETERY in U.10.d. Ammunition:- 75 MK.
2.0.a.m. to 4.0.a.m.	C/181. DOG TRENCH & TRIDENT ALLEY in U.21.b. Ammunition:- 75 rounds.	M.T.M.	A/181. CROISILLES-HENDECOURT Road in U.16.b. Ammunition:- 50 rounds.
4.0.a.m. to Dawn.	Infantry Patrols.	Machine Guns.	D/181. Railway in U.11.c. Ammunition. 10 M.

23.2.18.

Mark
Lieut., R.F.A.
A/Adjutant, Left Group, 59th D.A.

SECRET.

LEFT GROUP, 59th D.A.

NIGHT FIRING.

25/26th Feb.

Period.	ZONE A.	ZONE B.	ZONE C.
6.0.p.m. to 10.0.p.m.	C/181. VULCAN ALLEY & Sunken Rd. in U.15.c. Ammunition:- 50 rounds.	M.T.Ms.	D/181. SPANIEL ALLEY in U.16.b. Ammunition:- 15 EX.
10.0.p.m. to 2.0.a.m.	Infantry Patrols.	Machine guns.	D/181. U.10.d.9.9. Dug-outs & trench. Ammunition:- 10 EX.
2.0.a.m. to Dawn.	Infantry Patrols.	A/181. Trench Junction in U.15.b.90.60. and HOOP TRENCH. W.N.T. Ammunition:- 75 rounds.	B/181. X. Rds. & Tracks in U.10.d. Ammunition:- 75 rds.

Ammunition:- 18-prs. 60% A.X. 40% A.   4.5" Hows. 100% EX.

Mack
/Adjutant, LEFT Group, 59th D.A.
Lieut.R.F.A.

24th February, 1918..

SECRET.

LEFT GROUP 59th D.A..

NIGHT FIRING.
26/27th Feb.

Period.	ZONE A.	ZONE B.	ZONE C.
Dusk to 10.0.p.m.	Infantry Patrols.	Machine Guns.	D/181. Railway in U.16.b. and U.10.d. Ammunition 15 rds.
10.0.p.m. to midnight.	C/181. DOG LANE U.21.b. Ammunition. 75 rounds.	H.T.4s.	A/181. Road & tracks in U.10.o. Ammunition. 75 rds.
Midnight to Dawn.	Infantry Patrols.	Machine Guns. C/181. New work in U.16.c. from U.16.c.82.35. to U.16.c.85.40. Ammunition. 50 rounds.	D/181. UB2.11, 10. Ammunition. 10 rounds.

Ammunition:- 18-pdrs. 60% AX.
40% A.
4.5" Hows. 100% K.

H Howlan
Lieut. R.F.A.
A/Adjutant, Left Group, 59th D.A..

25th February, 1918..

Left Group 59th D.A.

NIGHT FIRING.
27/28th Feb.

Period.	ZONE A.	ZONE B.	ZONE C.
Dusk to 1.0.a.m.	Infantry Patrols.	C/181. COPSE TRENCH in U.10.d. Ammunition 70 rounds.	A/181. Roads & Railways in U.10.d. Ammunition:- 70 rounds.
1.0.a.m. to 3.0.a.m.	A/181. X Roads & Railway Alley in U.21.b. Ammunition 50 rounds.	H.T.M.	D/181. Sunken Rd. in U.11.c.& b Ammunition 10.RX.
3O.a.m. to Dawn.	NIHIL		D/181. Cellar HEUDICOURT U.11.c.0b.0b. Ammunition 10 RX.

Ammunition:- 18-pdrs. 60% A.X.
4.5". 40% A.
2" 10" 15% H.E.

L Shaw Lieut. F.A.
A/Adjutant, Left Group, 59th D.A.

40th Divisional Artillery.

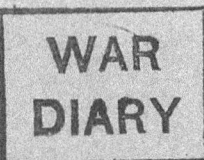

178th BRIGADE.

ROYAL FIELD ARTILLERY

MARCH 1918

WAR DIARY.

178 Bde R.F.A.

In the Field.

1918 March 1st	B/178 shelled by guns of many calibres; general increase of artillery activity along the line.
– 2nd	Nothing to report.
– 3rd	C.O., Adjutant and Sigs. Officer of relieving brigade, 152 Bde R.F.A. 34th Divn. arrived, the group becoming left group of 34th DA at 2 a.m. 2 sections for btys. were relieved and proceeded to wagon lines. A and C/178 assisted in a raid by group on our recent left.
– 4th	The 2 sections relieved yesterday proceeded to rest billets in SOUASTRE. Remainder of Bde. and HQs were relieved and proceeded to wagon lines.
– 5th	Remainder of brigade moved to SOUASTRE.
– 6th	A, B and C/178 are in SOUASTRE, as well as HQs. D/178 at BAYENCOURT. A, B and C are satisfied with their billets, D are not.
– 7th	Conference of BCs was held and training scheme for Bde. arranged.
– 8th	G.O.C. Divnl. Arty. was inspected by GOC IV Corps. He appeared to be satisfied. The weather is excellent.
– 9th	Colonel Parsons and BCs proceeded on a reconnaissance of the IV Corps front.
– 10th	Church parade at 10.30 a.m.

WAR DIARY.

In the Field. 1918
March 11th — The Divl. Band and Troupe gave a performance at 8pm in the village. Such was much appreciated by the audience.

— 12th — Advance parties proceeded by motor lorry to S17c to arrange about billetting the Bde; SISe however than their proper destination and the mistake was rectified. Tents were put up here & the Bde. arrived from SOUASTRE at midnight.

— 13th — Throughout the previous night our artillery was extremely active breaking up a German attack which did not materialise.

— 14th — Nothing to report. The weather is still very fine.

— 15th — Nothing to report.

— 16th — Nothing to report.

— 17th — The 178 Bde having challenged the 181 Bde to a football match and two legs of a rubber, were beaten in all three.

— 18th —
— 19th — } Nothing particular to report. The training continues; work in the morning and
— 20th —   football in the afternoon.

WAR DIARY

In the Field
1918
March 21st — The enemy attacked on a front extending from BULLECOURT to LA FERE. His preliminary bombardment commenced at 5 am and the first infantry attacks between 9 and 9.30. At the same time he systematically shelled back areas with HV guns, one 3 three areas being the field in which the Bde. was encamped. At 1 am. the Bde. received orders to go into action near MORY, in B 29 (sheet 57C). On arrival however, the positions were thought to be too close to the front line, and batteries took up new positions in B14 and 15. By the night the enemy was in possession of ECOUST, LONGATTE, NOREUIL and LAGNICOURT, and had captured many forward guns in these places. The HQs are in a hut on the ERVILLERS—HAMELINCOURT road, in B15B, and the Battery wagon lines near GOMIECOURT, in A23.

22nd — The attack was fairly quiet. During the day the enemy continued his advance and captured VRAUCOURT and VAULX—VRAUCOURT, and was on the outskirts of ST. LEGER. Our infantry are holding the Army line, but they have suffered very heavy casualties and there are several gaps in the line. By the evening the enemy was nothing his way round to MORY, thus threatening the right flank of the batteries; accordingly during the night they moved out and went into action in A24 c and D, at TRIANGLE COPSE. In the early hours of the morning Bde. HQs moved to BEHAGNIES , so as to be in touch with General Campbell 120 Inf. Bde.

Army Form C. 2118.

WAR DIARY
or
INTELLIGENCE SUMMARY.
(Erase heading not required.)

Instructions regarding War Diaries and Intelligence Summaries are contained in F. S. Regs., Part II. and the Staff Manual respectively. Title pages will be prepared in manuscript.

Place	Date	Hour	Summary of Events and Information	Remarks and references to Appendices
Field	March 23rd 1918	At 7am	HQs moved to GOMIECOURT. The situation did not undergo much change during the day. The Bde. were acting in OP in ERVILLERS and engaging favourable targets.	
	-24-		In change on our front. The enemy is advancing rapidly in the South. Orders were received at midnight that (?) he has reached a line COMBLES – MORVAL – LES BOEUFS. He was taking a northward Bfth right flank Bth Third Army. Shortly after midnight the divn. on our left was driven back and our front line was withdrawn to the East edge of ERVILLERS. At about 7 a.m. A and D/178 retired to positions behind the ACHIET-BOISLEUX railway (in A27), A after two batteries later in the morning head received that the enemy had broken through (At about information the direction of ACHIET.) In the afternoon the enemy shelled the area in which the Batteries were, and they retired gradually towards the COURCELLES – ABLAINZEVELLE road, their wagon lines being close behind. A Stole Line. Inannsile Colonel Parsons remained at GOMIECOURT CHATEAU with the 120 Inf. Bde. until the afternoon, then he rejoined the rest Bth Bde and the HQs were established in a hut just West of COURCELLES about A 15.	
	-25-			

INTELLIGENCE SUMMARY.

(Erase heading not required.)

Place	Date	Hour	Summary of Events and Information	Remarks and references to Appendices
Field	March 26th 1918		In the early hours of the morning the HQs moved to ABLAINZEVELLE and the batteries to positions immediately West of the BUCQUOY—AYETTE road. At about 9am the infantry were seen to be retiring from the railway line, which they were supposed to be holding, through ABLAINZEVELLE, and the batteries consequently were withdrawn to QUESNOY FARM, F14 (sht 57D), during a section the in close liaison with the infantry. These sections performed some extremely good work on enemy infantry between LO EAST WOOD and ABLAINZEVELLE. Meanwhile Colonel Parsons had left ABLAINZEVELLE to be in liaison with the 25th Inf. Bde., and the HQs left the village as our infantry were lining the road to BUCQUOY to fire at enemy infantry who were appearing in the direction of ACHIET; they proceeded to ESSARTS as ordered, but found themselves out of touch with the rest of the Bde. became Colonel Parsons did not go to the 25th Inf. Bde. but to some other Bde. to which we were all attached. The HQs accordingly attached themselves to Col. Scarlett, 151 Bde RFA, and remained with them at HANNESCAMPS until discovered by Captain Stephens in the evening. Orders were received for the Bde. It was incidentally discovered in the evening that orders had been given for the Bde. to march to HABARCQ, to form a Divisional Reserve under VI Corps. Accordingly Colonel Parsons rejoined HQs at HANNESCAMPS.	

INTELLIGENCE SUMMARY.

(Erase heading not required.)

Place	Date	Hour	Summary of Events and Information	Remarks and references to Appendices
Field	1918 March 27th	2 a.m.	At 2 a.m. the Bde. set out for KABARCQ, via MONCHY-AU-BOIS — RANSART — BELLACOURT — BEAUMETZ — WANQUETIN. Bdr. pit outside BEAUMETZ — orders were received from that the Bde. was to remain at BEAUMETZ. On receipt of fresh orders the Bde. B/f BEAUMETZ at 2 p.m. and X marched to BLAIREVILLE here Colonel Parsons met Bes and R.Os and went forward to reconnoitre battery positions in S8. When all arrangements had been made the orders were cancelled, and the batteries retired to their wagon lines in R33, and battery staffs and H Qs proceeded to SHRAPNEL CORNER to await further orders. At midnight these last counter-orders were themselves cancelled, and the batteries went into action in their selected positions, and the H Qs established themselves in a hut about X6A, in the outskirts of FICHEUX.	
	28th		The weather was bitter, & they were quiet. The Bde. is reinforcing the 74th, being left group guards D.A., and its front is roughly BOIRY- BECQUERELLE — BOYELLES. Our infantry are holding BOISLEUX ST MARC — BOISLEUX AU MONT. Lt. Col. C.T. Victory Cmdg. 74th Bde. is commanding the Group.	

WAR DIARY

In the Field

14.8
March 29th Colonel Parsons was slightly wounded in the foot. Enemy shelled area of battery positions vigorously with 5.9s in the afternoon. Major Wilkes took over command of the Bde.

— 30th — The enemy made three determined attacks on our lines in the morning. Our artillery fire completely demolished one of these, wiping out these battalions which attempted to attack on a frontage of one company. Brig.-Gen. Lord Henry Seymour, comdg. 3rd Guards Bde. expressed his gratitude to OC Bde. for this piece of work: "There is no doubt," he said, "that by sheer weight of numbers the enemy would have penetrated our line had it not been for the prompt and effective support given by your guns. The OC 1st Battn. Grenadier Guards joins with me in asking you to express my great gratitude to all ranks." While firing this SOS, Lt. Mann, 2/178 was killed, Major Cole wounded, 2 Lts. Beshmer Bygger and Dunbar slightly wounded. About 3 men were killed and 20 wounded. Enemy planes were flying very low over the battery positions. Bde. this bombardment was in progress. In the evening A, B and C/178 moved to new positions in Y6 and 12.

E. Campbell Ewart A/Lt
for Adjt. 178 Bde. RFA

— 31st — Nothing to report.

40th Divisional Artillery.

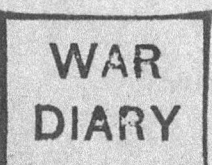

178th BRIGADE.

ROYAL FIELD ARTILLERY

APRIL 1918

176 Battery

Army Form C. 2118.

WAR DIARY
or
INTELLIGENCE SUMMARY.
(Erase heading not required.)

Instructions regarding War Diaries and Intelligence Summaries are contained in F. S. Regs., Part II. and the Staff Manual respectively. Title pages will be prepared in manuscript.

Place	Date	Hour	Summary of Events and Information	Remarks and references to Appendices
Field	1918 April 1	8 p.m.	Hostile planes are very active, constantly flying low over our lines and battery positions.	
	- 2		C/178 came under the command of Right Group Canadian Artillery.	
			Nothing to report.	
	- 3		Nothing to report.	
	- 4	6 p.m.	Major T. McGowan, A/78, took over command of the Bde.	
	- 5		2 Lt. P. G. Saul posted to D/178.	
	- 6		Nothing to report.	
	- 7		2 Lt. T. L. T. W. Catling posted to A/178.	
	- 8		Nothing to report.	
	- 9		The weather is becoming very misty, barometer low. The enemy sent over a good number of gas shells near battery positions during the day.	
	- 10		Visibility very bad owing to fog. Nothing to report.	
	- 11		Nothing to report.	
	- 12	midday	Advanced parties proceeded to GOUY-EN-ARTOIS to arrange about billets for the Bde. which was to be relieved this and the following night by 72nd A.F.A. Brigade, but to retain command at 6 p.m. and the Bde. remains where it is.	

WAR DIARY
INTELLIGENCE SUMMARY

Army Form C. 2118.

178 Bde R.F.A.

Place	Date	Hour	Summary of Events and Information	Remarks and references to Appendices
Field	1918 April 13	7 p.m.	C/178 Bde R.F.A. (having pulled out the previous night and proceeded to Boyy) came back and reoccupied a position in S.1.B. (sheet 51B). This battery now comes under the command of Major Bartleman, and 178 Bde and C/181 form a sub group B.Bn left Group.	
—	14	Night	The Guards infantry were relieved by the 2nd Division; their artillery still remains with us. Nothing to report.	
—	15			
—	16	8.30 a.m.	Batteries commenced firing counter preparation, immediately succeeded by S.O.S.	
		10.30 to 11.20 a.m. midday	Barrage put down on sunken road BOYELLES—BOISLEUX ST MARC. S.O.S. fired.	
		2.30 p.m.	Information was received that the enemy had gained a foot in our front line in S.18c. During the S.18 afternoon we fired S.O.S., sometimes full rate, sometimes half rate. In the evening it was ascertained that the enemy had got possession of our front line in S.12 and S.18, but though several times during the day we were informed that the infantry were about to attack to regain the lost trenches, but no action appeared to be developing. No reliable information could be obtained from the infantry at any time during the day.	

Army Form C. 2118.

WAR DIARY
or
INTELLIGENCE SUMMARY.
(Erase heading not required.)

Place	Date	Hour	Summary of Events and Information	Remarks and references to Appendices
Field	April 17		Nothing to report.	
	18		It is now confirmed that we have regained the portion of trench lost on the 16th inst., though the manner in which this was effected is still obscure.	
		10 am	Conference of brigade commanders held at 60 DA HQs at the Château, BRETENCOURT.	
		6 pm	Bde HQs moved to the Mairie, RANSART, & BC (sheet 51E) in order to be near the Bde HQs of 5th Tf. Bde 12nd Div. which we are covering. 178 Bde., with D/281, now becomes Centre Group to DA, the 74 Bty's to under the command of Lt.Col. C.F. Vickery, being Left Group, and the 155 A FA Bde; with T Bty RHA, and C/281, from under the command of Lt.Col. R.G. Finlayson, being Right Group.	
	19		Nothing to report.	
	20		Hostile planes were more active today than for some time past. Hostile artillery shelled RANSART and surrounding area little lately with HE and gas during the evening. The battery areas received a good deal of attention from the enemy guns during the night time. Practically no damage however has yet been done.	
	21		Battery positions were shelled last night fairly heavily with gas and HE; no damage done. Lieut. E.A. Bushman 1A/178 has been awarded the M.C. for valuable services rendered during the recent operations. In the same battery Sergt. T. Road has been awarded the M.M., and Sergt. A.Y. Osborn, C/178 has also received the M.M.	

178 Bde R 7 a

WAR DIARY
INTELLIGENCE SUMMARY.
(Erase heading not required.)

Place	Date	Hour	Summary of Events and Information	Remarks and references to Appendices
Field	1918 Mar 22		An arrangement has been made whereby one 4.5 how battery (D/178) and one 18 pr battery (C/178) may be called upon by the heavy gunners to carry out counter-battery shoots that are within their range.	
	23		The enemy carried out concentrations on MOYENNEVILLE at various times during the day. Lt. W. J. Salkeld left D/178 to proceed on a month's course of instruction at M.A.A.4. Considerable activity on the part of enemy's artillery during last night and today. During the night it shelled back areas pretty thoroughly with gas and HE.	
	24		Nothing to report. A very foggy day.	
	25		Nothing to report.	
	26		Another foggy day. Reports show that our harassing fire is extremely disconcerting to the enemy; it apparently is causing some casualties and much annoyance to him.	
	27		Nothing to report.	
	28		2 Lt. E. J. Bond posted to D/178. Hostile planes were rather more active, and some bombs were dropped on back areas during the evening.	
	29		2 Lt. P. M. Soul was slightly wounded while at the OP and retired to hospital. A conference of Group Commanders was held at left front HQs at BLAIREVILLE at which many fronts of interest were discussed, among them the siting of AT guns and short shooting by 18-pdrs.	
	30	10.30		
		4.30 PM		

WAR DIARY
INTELLIGENCE SUMMARY.

(Erase heading not required)

178 Bn RFA
178 Bn RFA
Vol 24

Place	Date	Hour	Summary of Events and Information	Remarks and references to Appendices
Field	19.18 2 Aug 1		Visibility bad owing to mist.	
	-2		A very 1st fine day; a marked increase in hostile artillery activity.	
	-3		Hostile artillery again very active; battery positions were shelled persistently throughout the day by 5.9's, the only damage inflicted being one man k.g. slightly wounded and one round of ammunition damaged.	
	-4		Battery positions again shelled. 2nd Lt Dix Clakland posted to C/178. T.S:	
	-5		Fairly hostile aerial activity, but their AA guns were more than usually in evidence. Weather very wet. Hostile artillery less active.	
	-6	9.27 pm	SOS signal from left battalion; 9.45 slow rate of fire, and 9 sp/gun fire. No information of a hostile action could be obtained from the infantry. So did not seen to have SOSetter; the enemy had attempted to raid our trenches on SOS. All that was certain was that a barrage had been put down in front and support line 7th left battalion. It was SOS even possible to ascertain whether the SOS rocket was sent up or not, since the infantry themselves appeared uncertain whether they had sent it up, and an attempt up did not prove any rocket at all.	

Army Form C. 2118.

WAR DIARY
or
INTELLIGENCE SUMMARY.
(Erase heading not required.)

178th Bde R.F.A.

Place	Date	Hour	Summary of Events and Information	Remarks and references to Appendices
Field	May 7		Apparently the enemy attempted to raid our trenches last night but did not succeed. Hostile artillery fairly quiet. The day was very fine. S.A. Lt-Delahaye posted to B/178. During last night and this early morning our artillery bombarded enemy trenches suspected of containing troops and put down gas with many Bo YELLES and the enemy bombardment in order to frustrate any concentrations or any night time raid for an attack. arrangements	
	-8			
	-9		The fine weather continues. Hostile artillery again quiet, but their planes were very active.	
	-10		Nothing to report.	
	-11		Atmospheric conditions being excellent for the purpose, the enemy carried out a heavy bombardment with mustard gas of an area about 2000 yds square North and North-East of HENDECOURT (sheet 51c). The fire from 3pm to about midnight, of many arts & fire; average rate of fire being about 500 rounds per hour. The large majority of shells	
	-12		were from 4.2 howrs, a few being from 5.9 how. Lt: N. Reed and Lt Brungfield posted to D/178 from 4 to Divnl. TMS.	

Army Form C. 2118.

178 Bde RFA

WAR DIARY
INTELLIGENCE SUMMARY.
(Erase heading not required.)

Instructions regarding War Diaries and Intelligence Summaries are contained in F. S. Regs., Part II. and the Staff Manual respectively. Title pages will be prepared in manuscript.

Place	Date	Hour	Summary of Events and Information	Remarks and references to Appendices
Field	May 13	12 noon	Billeting parties proceeded to FOSSEUX (shut S10) and each battery arranged to take over the billets of the corresponding battery of the 155 Army Brigade (Colonel R.G. Finlayson) Bde have been in rest at this place meanwhile. Colonel Finlayson and his Sigs. Officer proceeded to RANSART and were shown over battery positions, OPs etc.	
	14		During last night 2 sections per battery were relieved by corresponding batteries of the 155 A.B. and proceeded to their wagon lines. During the morning these sections and the wagon lines (less limbers per bty - being left for the remaining section) moved to FOSSEUX. HQs arrived at the village at about 8 pm.	
	15		The remaining section of each battery having pulled out of action last night to their wagon lines, moved to FOSSEUX during the morning. The 151st Bde. RFA is at HAUTEVILLE and the two Brigades are on callable reserve at one hour's notice between the hours of 8 am and 1 pm., and 3 hours' notice between 1 pm and 8 pm.	
	16		Colonel, 2 i/c, Brigade and R. Adjt., with battery commanders reconnoitred battery positions and OPs in the neighbourhood of POMMIER and BIENVILLERS-AU-BOIS (sheet 57.D.)	
	17		Nothing to report. The weather is extraordinarily fine.	
	18		Officers of the Brigade are busy reconnoitring battery positions for the further and Red Line + more particularly in the neighbourhood of POMMIER and MONCHY-AU-BOIS	
	19	10 am	Church parade was held in a field by the chateau, + medals won recently by Brig. + other members of the Brigade were afterwards presented by Brig. Gen. Palmer.	Major H. B. Burnaby 6/178 has been awarded the M.C.

Army Form C. 2118.

178 Bde RFA

WAR DIARY
or
INTELLIGENCE SUMMARY.
(Erase heading not required.)

Instructions regarding War Diaries and Intelligence Summaries are contained in F. S. Regs., Part II. and the Staff Manual respectively. Title pages will be prepared in manuscript.

Place	Date	Hour	Summary of Events and Information	Remarks and references to Appendices
Fall	May 20	4 am	Orders were received from VI Corps that the Brigade was to stand to and be prepared to move off at a moment's notice. At 8 am orders were received from the DA for the Brigade to move to the place afforested in readiness (neighbourhood of La Cauchie) in readiness. This was merely for test purposes, and see the Brigade had been detailed (with the C.R.A.) it returned to FOSSEUX. The 3rd Brigade had left FOSSEUX and there are now, I myself, 5th etc.	
	-21		The weather continues fine, very fine. Inter-battery football matches have commenced, for which there is a small piece of ground the NE of the village.	
	-22		The J.O.C. DA. inspected the horses of the Brigade; he was not satisfied with their condition	
	-23	6.30 p.m.	A boxing competition was held, by arrangement of the officers of C battery; it provided excellent sport.	
	-24		A very wet day.	
	-25		Some sports on horseback were held in the afternoon; flat races, hurdle races, wrestling and tugs of war.	
		7 pm	The finals of the boxing were fought, and prizes distributed by Colonel Chapman	

178 Bde R.F.A.

War Diary.

In the Field	May 26	10 am	Church parade was held in a field outside the village.
		3 pm	The Corps Commander inspected the Brigade and some of the horse lines. Advanced parties met the Staff Captain at the Town Major's Office, HUMBERCOURT, to arrange the billets for the Brigade.
	27	9 am	The Brigade left FOSSEUX for HUMBERCOURT.
	28	9 am	Colonel Hickman and the Adjutant proceeded to reconnoitre the positions that the Brigade will take over, at the relief, from the 165 Bde. R.F.A.
	29	9 am	The Orderly Officer and Signals Officer went up to the new H.Q.s to complete the arrangements for relief and returned to HUMBERCOURT in the evening. 2 sections per battery took over from their corresponding batteries after dusk.
	30	9 am	Command passed from the 165 Bde R.F.A. to the 178 Bde R.F.A. at 12 noon; the 181 Bde at the same taking over from the 170 Bde. The respective Bde. H.Q.s we situated at E.5.D.25.30 and E.5.B.60.90. The 181 Bde. H.Q.s covering the 3rd Gds Bde. H.Q.s, the 178 Bde being a sub-group, of the Right Army Guards Divisional Artillery. The 178 Bde battery positions are in Squares F1, 2, 7 and 9, in the valley between A DINEFER WOOD and QUESNOY FARM. The remaining section per battery came into action after dusk. Wagon lines are at ST. AMAND, but all the batteries except A have advanced limber lines close at hand towards MONCHY AU- Bois. The day was fairly quiet, but between 9·15 and 9·45 pm a heavy S.O.S. barrage was
	31		

178 Bde RFA
Vol 25

SECRET

1918

War Diary.

In the Field

June 1. 3.5 am. — A fairly heavy barrage was put down on the front system & the 2nd
of this Zone, which gradually shifted Southwards and finally ceased when it had
arrived at ABLAINZEVELLE. At the same time a smoke barrage was put
down between AYETTE and DOUCHY. No infantry action developed, but as
communications with the infantry were out the Brigade fired SOS of a slow
rate, followed by Annihilating Fire, until it was ascertained that it was
not necessary. The barrage ceased at 6.5 AM.
Hostile artillery was less active than usual during the day.

— 2. Hostile artillery was very active between 12.15 pm and 3 pm on the MONCHY
SWITCH SYSTEM in E1 (sheet 57 D), bombarding it fairly heavily at an irregular
rate of fire with 5. 9s.
Hostile artillery was much quieter than usual. Visibility was excellent in
the evening.

— 4. 178 Bde HQs proceeded into rest at St Amand; the 181 HQs. taking over command
of the group. Command passed at 6pm yesterday.
— 5. Nothing to report.
— 6. Nothing to report.

WAR DIARY
or
INTELLIGENCE SUMMARY.
(Erase heading not required.)

Army Form C. 2118.

178 Bde RFA

Place	Date	Hour	Summary of Events and Information	Remarks and references to Appendices
Field	June 7		Guards Division was relieved by the 2nd Division	
	-8		Hostile artillery is becoming quieter though his TMs in A BEAINZAVELLE	
		10 am	frequently and inconvenience and casualties from Infantry	
			to DA took men forward from Guards DA	
	-9		Nothing to report	
	-10		Nothing to report	
	-11		Nothing to report, though TMs again fairly active	
	-12		Nothing to report	
	-13		An Infantry relief being suspected our Batteries fired a special programme	
			to deal with the situation	
	-14		Nothing to report.	
	-15		A divisional relief to the enemy's lines was suspected and the	
			attempt for august firing was increased accordingly	
	-16		90 Bde HOs moved back into the line in the evening.	
			178 Bde HOs took over command of the group at 11 am.	
	-17		c/p/81 has moved out its reserve at POMMIER (Sheet 57c) as an anti-	
			Tank battery to be employed either against tanks in an attack, or otherwise as	
			the situation might demand	

Army Form C. 2118.

178 Bde RFA

WAR DIARY
or
INTELLIGENCE SUMMARY.
(Erase heading not required.)

Place	Date	Hour	Summary of Events and Information	Remarks and references to Appendices
Field	June 18		The area surrounding A/178 was shelled heavily with 5.9s from 9am to 12-30pm; one gun was damaged and sent to the I.O.M. for repairs. Otherwise hostile artillery was quiet.	
	-19		Hostile artillery was fairly quiet, but about 800 rounds 77mm or 18-pdr, half the latter, were fired intermittently throughout the day in F20 B. The MPI was the position of the forward section of A 181, but no damage was done.	
	-20		A large number of Blue and Yellow Cross shells were fired during the early morning into the valley South of QUESNOY FARM, and a few more during the day.	
	-21		Hostile artillery rather active throughout the day, especially in registering to the neighbourhood of battery positions with air bursts HE.	
	-22		One section for battery was relieved by the corresponding sections of the batteries of the 2nd Divisional Artillery during the night and proceeded to their new positions. A & B and C/178 are attached to the right group; 32 nd D.A.; D/178 to the centre group; and C/178 to the left Bde, 32 nd Division. A, B and D are in positions in the same area as they were in before the last rest, covering HAMELIN COURT and Mc KENNEVILLE.	
	-23	5pm	Brigade HQs. moved to Château BEAU METZ; here they will be, n.d. of action, till the remaining 2 sections for btty. were relieved and came into action within [further action was posted.] after dusk.	

Army Form C. 2118.

178 Bde RFA.

WAR DIARY
or
INTELLIGENCE SUMMARY.
(Erase heading not required.)

Instructions regarding War Diaries and Intelligence Summaries are contained in F. S. Regs., Part II. and the Staff Manual respectively. Title pages will be prepared in manuscript.

Place	Date	Hour	Summary of Events and Information	Remarks and references to Appendices
Field	June 24		Resting & refit.	
	25		} Resting & refit.	
	26			
	27			
	28			
	29			
	30			

Army Form C. 2118.

WAR DIARY
*
INTELLIGENCE SUMMARY.
(Erase heading not required.)

178 Bde RFA

9/8 26

Place	Date	Hour	Summary of Events and Information	Remarks and references to Appendices
Field	July 1st		Nothing to report.	
	2nd	2pm	A Gymkhana was held by the 1st Guards Brigade at La Bazèque. *Sheet SIC	*Sheet SIC
			178 strongly represented in the open events.	
	3rd	2·30pm	The "eliminating trials" for the Transport show (open to VI Corps) took place in a field near	
			Sault. C/181 1st and C/178 second in battery section competition; No 2 section DAC	
			won 1st, No 4 section second in the DAC competition	
	4th		Nothing to report.	
	5th	"	"	
	6th	"	"	
	7th	"	"	
	8th	"	"	
	9th	"	Nothing to report.	
	10th	2·30pm	The 45th Division won everything that was open to them in the Corps transport show.	
			C/178 won the 1st prize for the battery section competition, as I saw DAC won 1st and	
			No 2, 2nd, and No 1 Bty Divnl Train won 1st	
	11th		Nothing to report.	

WAR DIARY
or
INTELLIGENCE SUMMARY.
(Erase heading not required.)

Army Form C. 2118.

Place	Date	Hour	Summary of Events and Information	Remarks and references to Appendices
In Field	Feb 12th		Lt. Col. T. The Groven proceeded on leave to the United Kingdom.	
	13th		Nothing to report.	
	14th		Nothing to report.	
	15th		Nothing to report.	
	16th		BEAUMETZ was heavily shelled by a 5.9 HV gun throughout the day.	
	17th		Nothing to report.	
	18th		Nothing to report.	
	19th		BEAUMETZ again received a great deal of attention from a HV gun.	
	20th		Nothing to report.	
	21st		"	
	22nd		"	
	23rd		Major S.M. Oakes, C/172 proceeded to the United Kingdom on 5 days' special leave.	
	24th		Nothing to report.	
	25th		"	
	26th		"	

Army Form C. 2118.

WAR DIARY
or
INTELLIGENCE SUMMARY.
(Erase heading not required.)

Place	Date	Hour	Summary of Events and Information	Remarks and references to Appendices
Field	July 27th		Lt. Col. T. McGowan returned from leave. Getting to report.	
	-28th			
	-29th		Major S.M. Brooks C/178 returned from leave. Getting to report.	
	-30th			
	-31st		The Bde. took over from the 232nd & 27A Bde., Bde. HQs moving into BLAIREVILLE WOOD, R35 c05 95 # and taking over command at 12 noon. One section per battery relieved during last night, the remaining two during the night 31st – 1st August. For the present, B/178 is still under our command, but A, B and D/178 form a sub group of the Right Group. Left (59#) Divn. The main battery positions are in the FICHEUX area, including the ground between the village eastwards towards the railway. One anti-tank gun at S4A.85.65. is manned by a battery. There are also forward guns or sections for each battery.	# Sheet 51c

Aug 1918
178 Bde RFA
VOL 27

Army Form C. 2118

WAR DIARY
or
INTELLIGENCE SUMMARY
(Erase heading not required.)

Place	Date	Hour	Summary of Events and Information	Remarks and references to Appendices
In the field	Aug 1.		Nothing to report.	
	2.		Nothing to report.	
	3.	10 am	6/178 rejoined the Brigade, but died then became left Group 59th Division, covering 177th Infantry Brigade.	
	4.		The weather is extremely hot. Nothing to report.	
	5.		Nothing to report.	
	6.		Nothing to report.	
	7.		It is almost impossible to obtain any information concerning the enemy on this front; practically no movement is seen during the day, and 6 officers to hold his line which very few troops.	
	8.		Nothing to report.	
	9.		Nothing to report.	
	10.		Hostile Artillery slightly more active than usual on our front.	
	11.		Nothing to report.	
	12.		Nothing to report.	

Army Form C. 2118

WAR DIARY
or
INTELLIGENCE SUMMARY
(Erase heading not required.)

Instructions regarding War Diaries and Intelligence Summaries are contained in F.S. Regs., Part II. and the Staff Manual respectively. Title Pages will be prepared in manuscript.

Place	Date	Hour	Summary of Events and Information	Remarks and references to Appendices
In Field	Aug/13		nothing to report	
	14		— do —	
	15		nothing to report.	
	16		} nothing to report	
	17			
	18			
	19		} Nothing to report.	
	20			
	21		The Bdes. put down heavy barrages in support of an attack made by the Guards' Division on our right from 3.30am onwards throughout the morning. The attack resulted in the capture of HAMELINCURT and MOYENNEVILLE	Sheet 51B.
	22		The 5th and 58th A.T.A. Bdes. came into action in the Bde. area; the 70 Bde threw forming a group for these Bdes.	

WAR DIARY or INTELLIGENCE SUMMARY

Army Form C. 2118

Instructions regarding War Diaries and Intelligence Summaries are contained in F.S. Regs., Part II. and the Staff Manual respectively. Title Pages will be prepared in manuscript.

(Erase heading not required.)

Place	Date	Hour	Summary of Events and Information	Remarks and references to Appendices
In the Field	Aug 25	5 am	At 5 am the 57th Divn. attacked, preceded by a barrage from nine tanks, and accompanied by nine tanks. By 6.45 am the objectives, including the village of BOIRY-BECQUERELLE, had been gained. By the evening, the Canadians on the left were holding the ridge, a collection of trenches 500 yds. South of NEUVILLE VITASSE, but the village itself was still in the enemy's hands. During dark the Bde. moved up to the position in BOISLEUX AU MONT.	Sheet 51B
	-26	4.55 am	The 52nd Divn. attacked the HENIN HILL, carrying the position and advancing to the Hindenburg Line, but were prevented from entering it by a barrage which our howitzers were putting down on it. Our barrage was very accurate and had extremely satisfactory results. At dark the Bde. moved up to BOIRY WORKS, the Batteries being in astrile reserve. No further action was taken by the infantry during the day.	
	-25		The 52nd Divn. attacked the Hindenburg Line, and after the capture of MONCHY LE PREUX by the Canadians had been announced at 7 am, the 52nd (?) the line was in our hands from MONCHY to FONTAINE; and, resuming South by the infantry a battle-tank grid line & from MONCHY	
	-26	3 am		

Army Form C. 2118

WAR DIARY
or
INTELLIGENCE SUMMARY
(Erase heading not required.)

Place	Date	Hour	Summary of Events and Information	Remarks and references to Appendices
In the Field	Aug 27	9.30 am	At 9.30 am the 51st Divn. advanced to attack FONTAINE-LES-CROISILLES and CROISILLES. The barrage was apparently effective and FONTAINE was captured, but the stubborn resistance of enemy machine-gunners in CROISILLES prevented our troops from advancing in this direction. During the afternoon the 52rd Bde Brigade moved up and the reverse slope of the hill and an OP was established in a trench on the reverse slope of the hill overlooking the SENSEE VALLEY.	Sheet 51 B
	-28	12.30 pm	At 12.30 pm a barrage of two hours' duration was put down in support of an attack by the 57th Divn on HENDECOURT and RIEN COURT. Positions for batteries in the SENSEE VALLEY between FONTAINE and CROISILLES were reconnoitred during the afternoon, but A and B and D batteries moved down at dusk. There appears to be a pocket of the enemy holding out in the ravine of trenches on the crest 2000 yds East of CROISILLES. She sweep of the SENSEE VALLEY with their M.Gs. [illegible] and A and E Btys moved into positions close to the Hindenburg line. H.Qs are At dusk these Btl batteries moved at turns and turns straight down in the valley. close to the batteries in the HINDENBURG LINE.	

WAR DIARY
or
INTELLIGENCE SUMMARY

(Erase heading not required.)

Army Form C. 2118

Instructions regarding War Diaries and Intelligence Summaries are contained in F. S. Regs., Part II. and the Staff Manual respectively. Title Pages will be prepared in manuscript.

Place	Date	Hour	Summary of Events and Information	Remarks and references to Appendices
In the Field	Aug 29		The shefield last night by the infantry for an assault of them attack from 500 yds. West of UPTON WOOD & East of HENDECOURT and through BULLECOURT. Preceded by a barrage the 57th Divn. attacked the villages of HENDECOURT and RIENCOURT. They were successful at HENDECOURT, but apparently did not clear RIENCOURT following. On the flanks, the were held up by M.G. fire from CROW'S NEST. The situation round BULLECOURT is obscure. At dusk A and C Btties moved down little valley close to B and D. At 10am this exchanged with those of the 2/R Bde RFA (57 D/A), the 17 Bde leaving left Bde. Left group 5/6 & 3/A. The 181 Bde HQs remarks the same in these positions, but the S the grp. The batteries remained in these positions. The enemy pushed in troops moved down close to them in the valley last night and has established a ont of BULLECOURT and E COURT last night and has established a number of M.G. posts and snipers in the neighbourhood of STATION REDOUBT and in the crest between BULLECOURT and E COURT. There are however receiving the attention of our guns.	Sheet 51B HENDECOURT. they were told Sheet 51B
	Aug 30	1 pm		

Place	Date	Hour	Summary of Events and Information	Remarks and references to Appendices
In the Field	Sep 3		ECOUST and the village of BULLECOURT have been cleared of the enemy though he is still in some of the trenches to the South-East of the latter village.	
		5am–7am	A barrage was fired by the Bde. on trenches on the crest South East of BULLECOURT to enable the infantry (56 Divn) to gain possession of the crest. The operation was fairly successful, though till a later hour of the day the enemy was reported to be still in TANK AVENUE and TANK SUPPORT, trenches running along the top of the crest. During the afternoon positions were reconnoitred by BCs in the valley running South West from HENDECOURT to cover the DROCOURT – QUÉANT line. All positions were agreed upon on fact; & of course Jour artillery line.	

Army Form C. 2118.

14
178 BatRFA
M 28

WAR DIARY
or
INTELLIGENCE SUMMARY.
(Erase heading not required.)

Place	Date	Hour	Summary of Events and Information	Remarks and references to Appendices
In the Field	Sept 1.	6pm–7pm	To assist the 57th Division in their attack on HENDECOURT CHATEAU a creeping barrage was put down (containing a small percentage of smoke) commencing 500 yds East of BULLECOURT and retreating to a front with HENDENBURG Line 1000 yds. South of RIENCOURT. After this B and D batteries moved forward into positions in a valley 1000 yds. North West of BULLECOURT.	
	–2	5 a.m.	In order to mislead the enemy as to the extent of an attack, Shell limelight two or three miles North of SHE a 'false' barrage was put down on trenches South and South East of RIENCOURT. At 5.45 a.m. the same barrage was repeated, to support an infantry attack on the high ground between RIENCOURT and QUEANT. This barrage was continued till 10 a.m. The attack was successful. At the same time the Canadians on the left continued their advance over the ridge East of HENDECOURT. and the Division's right, but the troops immediately to our South were held up by M.G. fire. During the early morning Rde HQ's moved up into a position close to D battery, and later in the day went on to BULLECOURT, Shik A and C batteries advanced and took up positions on the BULLECOURT—HENDECOURT road.	

WAR DIARY
or
INTELLIGENCE SUMMARY.
(Erase heading not required.)

Army Form C. 2118.

Place	Date	Hour	Summary of Events and Information	Remarks and references to Appendices
In the Field	Sept 3		During the latter part of yesterday the enemy withdrew on the Canal du Nord line, leaving only a few machine gunners to cover his rear. The situation is known however, and no orders have been received for the Brigade to advance accordingly. During the early afternoon all the batteries moved out of the valley immediately West of QUEANT, and took up a sunken road north of the village.	Sketch 51C
	4		The XVII & Corps is now advancing on a one-Division frontage (that Division being the 63rd), which has advanced to the Canal du Nord, and is engaged in sapping the crossings from MOEUVRES to INCHY-EN-ARTOIS. The Guards Division (VI Corps) are moving north eastwards to make contact with the 63rd. The 52nd and 56th Divisions are behind the 63rd, protecting from the South. The 281 Bde. (Army) and immediately South East) QUEANT and PRONVILLE, in the HINDENBURG LINE is sufficiently PRONVILLE. The 178 Bde. is under the 281 Bde. (Grips), and is not in action. During the evening a few 157 Bde. (52nd Divn.), but is 4.5, 5.9 HV gun, and all the batteries moved casualties were inflicted in A Bty 4.5, 5.9 HV gun, and in positions further west of the valley. During the evening the batteries came into action in the area B/L HIRONDELLE R	
	5		valley (immediately West of QUEANT), and remained in positions of observation. The Bde. is now under the command of the 63rd D.A.	

Army Form C. 2118.

WAR DIARY
or
INTELLIGENCE SUMMARY.
(Erase heading not required.)

Instructions regarding War Diaries and Intelligence Summaries are contained in F. S. Regs., Part II. and the Staff Manual respectively. Title pages will be prepared in manuscript.

Place	Date	Hour	Summary of Events and Information	Remarks and references to Appendices
In the Field	Sept 6		All ranger lines were moved back into the area between CROISILLES and BULLECOURT (T 19 and 20). The enemy's artillery is very active, S.9 hours and HV guns firing at "B" the limit of their ranges on both forward and back areas. The 63rd DA has now been relieved by the 57th DA.	Sheet 51B
	7		This part of the battle front may now be said to have settled. Over troops are busily engaged in repairing roads, railways etc., bringing up ammunition and securing the water supply.	
	8		The enemy having abandoned a few guns in this area some Offr. Officers of E battery, Lts. Payne and Blundell and 2 Lt. Wood, have collected the scattered parts of those Brit Bat had been damaged and find all the ammunition they could find into the enemy's territory. This procedure has apparently caused him considerable annoyance and is be reflected by shelling the area Slowens he has observed the flash 8t4 being fired.	
	9	4.8 pm	The batteries moved up into action, slightly further forward, in an area 500-1000 yds. South of PRONVILLE.	

WAR DIARY
or
INTELLIGENCE SUMMARY.
(Erase heading not required.)

Army Form C. 2118.

Place	Date	Hour	Summary of Events and Information	Remarks and references to Appendices
In the Field	Sept 10		The situation is unchanged.	
	-11	6.15pm	A barrage was fired in support of an attack on the canal crossings from Inchy southwards. At the same time an attack was delivered on the VI Corps front on our right. The attack on our front was apparently successful, but severe resistance was met with north at the crossing nearest Inchy, and in the neighbourhood of Moeuvres.	
	-12	6.5pm	The enemy counter-attacked to regain possession of MOEUVRES. He was only partially successful, and did not drive us out of the village, but during the night a few men penetrated into the North Eastern part of it. SOS The Bde. fired on SOS lines from 6.6 to 6.36 pm.	
	-13		A few of the enemy appear to be still in MOEUVRES, but the infantry are gradually cutting them off.	
	-14		During the evening the batteries established advanced limber-lines in the Hirondelle valley west of QUEANT, in case of the need for a sudden move by the batteries.	Sheet 57c
	-15	10.30am	Casualties to between 20 and 30 horses were caused by 77m shells. They accordingly moved further away, in the direction of Bullecourt.	

WAR DIARY
or
INTELLIGENCE SUMMARY.
(Erase heading not required.)

Army Form C. 2118.

Place	Date	Hour	Summary of Events and Information	Remarks and references to Appendices
In the Field	Sept 16	4 pm	The Bde relieved the 285 Bde RFA, taking over command. Bde Left Group 57 DA. Sixth army orders, Bde 178 Bde, the 181 Bde, and two batteries of the 9th Brigade. The trks. are on the railway running above the Hindenburg Support line. North of PRONVILLE (V28 D11)*, and the batteries are at the INCHY-PRONVILLE valley, within 1500 yds. of the Western outskirts of INCHY (D11D and D12C).* The enemy's guns were very active throughout the day (HE and gas, chiefly Blue Cross, combined), and the batteries were heavily shelled. Men coming into action. Dak Cleland, e battery 178 Bde, performed a very gallant act in carrying a wounded gunner through a barrage to place of safety.	*Sheet 51B SE *Sheet 57B SE
	—17	10.30 am	At 10.30 am the enemy halted and wiped out one four tubs immediately south of MOEUVRES. The 9th Bde, fired on SOS lines from 10.35 to 11.8 am.	
		6.15 pm	At 6.15 pm the enemy attacked to gain possession of MOEUVRES. He was apparently successful, and by nightfall had driven our troops back to the extreme Western edge of the village. Coincident with the enemy's barrage in MOEUVRES and the surrounding trenches an exceedingly heavy burst of fire lasting for about 1/2 hour minutes, was put down on the battery positions. No personal casualties were sustained. My group fired on SOS lines at that assault and no casualties were sustained. 1/7/18 from 6.20 pm to 7.35 pm.	

WAR DIARY or INTELLIGENCE SUMMARY

Army Form C. 2118.

Place	Date	Hour	Summary of Events and Information	Remarks and references to Appendices
In the Field	Sept 18		The enemy's artillery was again very active with gas and H.E. The situation in MOEUVRES remains unchanged.	
	—19	2am 11.30 am	Enemy till 6.45 pm 4.5 hows Gas loaded MOEUVRES. 180 rounds per hour, and at 7 pm & we attacked the village and regained possession of it.	
	—20	6 am	At 6am the command of the Left Group passed to O.C. 286 Bde R.F.A. (Lt. Col. L.T.W. Robinson DSO R.F.A.). To Shorn A and C batteries 78th R.B. are attached for the rest of the day. Still B and D batteries come under the command of the 56th Bde R.F.A. (Right Group). The 81st Bde, in as well as two batteries 82th - 9th Bde, was meanwhile under the Right Group. This rearrangement is necessitated by the extension of the front covered by the Canadian Corps on our South. Shrd Lan was taken over the line to a point immediately North of MOEUVRES. During the evening the batteries were relieved by corresponding batteries of the 285 & Bde R.F.A. (Lt. Col. Cocker R.F.A.) and took up new positions about 2000 yds further South, to cover the front of the canal about 1000 yds South East of MOEUVRES. The Hrs. moved in to PRONVILLE - INCHY valley, and by 12 midnight had resumed command of the Bde, Shd then came under the 56th Bde (Right Group)	D17Q + 22A Sheet 57c

WAR DIARY
or
INTELLIGENCE SUMMARY.
(Erase heading not required.)

Army Form C. 2118.

Place	Date	Hour	Summary of Events and Information	Remarks and references to Appendices
To the Field	Sept 21	9.30pm	The Bde fired on SOS lines in response to signals. The enemy reached our line East of MOEUVRES and succeeded in entering it, but was thrown out by a counter-attack. Fire was stopped at 4.30 am.	
	22		The Bde fired on SOS lines, searching forward beyond the Canal, from 6.55 to 7.15 pm. The men ordered by group (5 Bde & Bde RFA) but the reason for it could not be discovered U.Col. A. Walker, RFA was attached to the Bde, and arrived at HQ in the morning. There he will live.	
	23	7.5 pm	The enemy having delivered an attack on the Canadians on our left, the alarm spread from front, and fire was opened on SOS lines, but afterwards it was stopped at 7.25pm after it had been ascertained that there was no need for it.	
	24		Fire was opened on SOS lines, slow rate, at 3.30pm, and ceased at 3.55 pm.	
	25	7.30 am	The enemy attempted to raid one of our posts and fire was opened on SOS lines	

WAR DIARY or INTELLIGENCE SUMMARY

Place	Date	Hour	Summary of Events and Information	Remarks and references to Appendices
In the Field	Sept 26		In the early morning the enemy penetrated into one of our posts North of MOEUVRES; fire was opened on him and drove him out. The 4 & 5 howitzers were engaged in heavy shelling of the enemy in front of MOEUVRES; fire was steady and fired 500 rounds during the day on the area in front of the Canal du Nord line, East of MOEUVRES. The howitzers have fired practically continuously, day and night, since the Bde. came into action in the vicinity valley, on the ruse of the month, and Officers, men, and horses are equally exhausted. In addition to the ammunition that is necessary for the day- and night- firing programmes and the regular SOSes a very large quantity has to be periodically in readiness at the battery position for the impending attack. The enemy's artillery was fairly active during the day.	

WAR DIARY
or
INTELLIGENCE SUMMARY
(Erase heading not required.)

Army Form C. 2118.

Place	Date	Hour	Summary of Events and Information	Remarks and references to Appendices
In the Field	Sept 27/17	5:20 a.m.	Zero hour for an attack by the British First and Third Armies. On this front the attack was divided into three phases. The first consisted of the advance of the 52nd and 63rd Divisions on the Hindenburg Support line; the second of the further advance of the 63rd on the ANNEUX — GRAINCOURT Spur; and the third of the attack by the 57th Division, coming through the 63rd, on a line running immediately east of FONTAINE NOTRE DAME and CANTAING. This was the intention, but in fact the attack was held up in front of MOEUVRES by machine guns for a considerable time, though the flanks passed forward according to plan. The first phase continued from zero to 3.+ 176, the second from 3.+ 176 to 3.+ 291, the third from 3.+ 291 to 3.+ 430. A creeping barrage was put down & from zero to 3.+ 124, covering the ground in a line between in all cases except the last. MOEUVRES and ANNEUX. At about 3.+ to one section of B battery	

Place	Date	Hour	Summary of Events and Information	Remarks and references to Appendices
7th Field Coy RE	5/1/17		and no section of D went forward with the intention of crossing the canal of trestle. They were unable, owing to machine-gun fire, and remained in the valley running South from MOEUVRES. Before $8/73$ + 121 the remainder of the guns had moved forward into this valley and were waiting to cross the canal. They should have been in action again by 3 + 210 namely to start the barrage for the attack on the third objective, which in fact was not needed because our infantry were still held up by MGs at the FACTORY on the main road. In the meanwhile Col. Inchgower and Major Sineton had gone forward onto the east side. Side looks down on the canal. At about half past six Major Sineton was killed by a M.G. bullet and Lt.Col. H.L. Walker over command though still dangerously. At 11.30 a.m. a bridge over the canal was made, though all the batteries / registered it was thrown, difficulty	

WAR DIARY
INTELLIGENCE SUMMARY

Army Form C. 2118.

Place	Date	Hour	Summary of Events and Information	Remarks and references to Appendices
In the Field	Sept 27 cont		came into action immediately west of the Hindenburg line (E22). Bde H.Qs. were established in the trench itself. The infantry were held up by M.Gs of the FACTORY, accordingly at a bombardment was put down on the place from 12.45 to 2.15 pm after which the Infantry advanced, and during the afternoon succeeded in taking all the ground up to FONTAINE and CANTAING (inclusive), with a fair number of prisoners. It was noticed that the batteries should move up into the valley between BOURLON WOOD and ANNEUX, but at dusk the enemy apparently counter-attacked and drove our troops back to the Eastern outskirts of ANNEUX. The situation therefore was not cleared at- The Bde. is now supporting the 17 & 72 Inf. Bde. (57th Division).	Sub Sheet 57c
	Sept 28		During the morning it was ascertained that our troops were East of FONTAINE and CANTAING and were in touch with the enemy in the ESCAUT Canal. accordingly advanced and took up positions	

WAR DIARY or INTELLIGENCE SUMMARY.

Army Form C. 2118.

Place	Date	Hour	Summary of Events and Information	Remarks and references to Appendices
In the field	Sept 28 Cont		in the valley two yards East of ANNEUX. The event of importance took place during the remainder of the day.	
	Sept 29		Orders were received that the Bde. should be attached to the 172 Inf. Bde. (57th Divn) in order that the artillery should be better able closely to support the infantry in their advance. Communication was established between the two Brigade HQs in the evening. B.G. Commanding the 172 Inf. Bde is Brig. Genl. C.B.G. Paynter DSO M.C. is in command of the 172 Inf. Bde.	
	Sept 30	At 5.30 a.m.	the Bde. fired a barrage in support of an attack by the 171 Inf. Bde. in two branches West and South West of Proville. Two sections of A/172 crossed the canal and came into action near Contigneul Mill, in Frs+. The infantry were unable to progress, but advance through PROVILLE & Sheet 57c. owing to M.G. fire from houses in the neighborhood. The remaining guns of the Bde. advanced during the morning and came into action between FONTAINE NOTRE DAME and LA FOLIE WOOD.	

WAR DIARY
or
INTELLIGENCE SUMMARY.
(Erase heading not required.)

Army Form C. 2118.

Place	Date	Hour	Summary of Events and Information	Remarks and references to Appendices
In the field	Sept 30 cont.	4pm	The Infantry advanced under cover of a barrage fired by the Bdes. and captured PROVILLE, with about 15 prisoners. Bdle the 71st and 72nd Inf. Btns. have suffered heavy casualties in today's fighting, almost entirely from machine guns concealed in houses, sunken roads etc. At about 5pm the two sections 8/A/78 came back across the canal d'Escaut and rejoined their other two guns in the valley. HQrs. were established in the Catacombs near the Church in FONTAINE NOTRE DAME. Major H.B. EMERTON, Capt B. MCLELLAND 6/78, and 2nd Lt. T.L.H.W. Cottingham have been Lt. T.S. Dick awarded the Military Cross.	

WAR DIARY
or
INTELLIGENCE SUMMARY.
(Erase heading not required)

Army Form C. 2118.

Place	Date	Hour	Summary of Events and Information	Remarks and references to Appendices
In the Field	Oct 1		From now onwards the French system of denoting time will be used in the British Armies.	Sheet 57B
			At 17.44 hours 170 Iny Bde (British) attacked with the intention of taking a trench running South West of the Faubourg St Sépulcre, and a barrage, at first creeping, subsequently stationary, was fired from 3000 & 3184. The attack was unsuccessful and the infantry returned to their original line, running through the middle of PROVILLE.	
			During the evening it was announced that our infantry had gained possession of the Faubourg de Paris, a group of houses on the CAMBRAI – RUMILLY Road. An O.P. has been established in a house by the railway station at FONTAINE NOTRE DAME, from which an excellent view can be obtained of CAMBRAI and the country behind it, though the view of our own particular front is somewhat obscured by trees. Lt. H. WEEKES has rejoined the Bde. and has ~~been posted to battery 178~~	
	2		~~The enemy are not in force in front of the Faubourg de Paris. At 18.00 the Bde fired a barrage to cover an attack by the infantry on this suburb, but the attack was unsuccessful. The enemy is still in occupation of the very active in the neighbourhood of la folie wood and artillery barrage~~ he does not seem to have many guns on the front, but is using them chiefly to harass the premises better full expert	
	3			
	4			

Army Form C. 2118.

WAR DIARY
or
INTELLIGENCE SUMMARY

(Erase heading not required.)

Place	Date	Hour	Summary of Events and Information	Remarks and references to Appendices
In the Field	Oct 5	—	The enemy's artillery was again very active on battery positions and neighbourhood. For the last three days one section of guns from each position north East of the Canal though caught and remained they are too far on screening of daylight, in order to fire on any special targets, the infantry has hardly been engaged.	
	6		Hostile artillery was again active. HV guns cause the majority of casualties, especially when they shoot at wagon lines. I shut there is a great number in this neighbourhood. The batteries there lost more than fifty horses since the same its three positions. Gas walters to personal have not been so heavy, but we are still negligible. Nothing to report.	
	7			
	8	4.30	The 2nd & 5 Division delivered an attack, in conjunction with the rest of the Third Army, with a view of pursuing SE from Hargnies on the first objective and the head of Bohain Seiche, Serainville, on the second.	Sket 57B

WAR DIARY
INTELLIGENCE SUMMARY
(Erase heading not required.)

Army Form C. 2118.

Place	Date	Hour	Summary of Events and Information	Remarks and references to Appendices
In the Field	Oct 8 cont		The Bde. field barrages in support of this attack, like those put down along A/178 Bde. confined itself to screening sabs screens, put down along the Southern edge of the Southern outskirts of CAMBRAI, extending from PROVILLE to RUE ST. LAZRE. The remaining batteries covered the advance from the CAMBRAI – ROMILLY road the second objective through NOYELLES SUR l'ESCAUT L battery, crossed across the Canal de l'Escaut 30 minutes after zero hour, C battery and came into action in a small valley immediately N E of ROMILLY. The other batteries followed to the same area. Considerable difficulty was found in crossing the Canal, though bridges on the Bde were length. One of the bridges built by our engineers B/178 C battery was crossing it, with the result that one gun and four horses were lost in the water. The enemy apparently observed the batteries coming into action and shelled them very heavily for some time, wounding 7 O.R's and about 30 O.R's amongst the Bde. B/178	Sheet 57B Sheet 57C Sheet 57B

2.Lt. W.R. BAILLIE 1 B/178

WAR DIARY
INTELLIGENCE SUMMARY

Army Form C. 2118.

Place	Date	Hour	Summary of Events and Information	Remarks and references to Appendices
NIERGNIES	Oct 8th 1918 cont.		The enemy counter attacked from the N.E. of NIERGNIES, using seven or eight tanks, and drove our infantry back to the first objective. They were forward with the infantry battalions the second. CAPT. BOSHMAN 1B/17, and LT. V.R. BLUNDELL C/78, therefore fired at two of the tanks and put one out of action. The enemy were then driven back and the infantry regained their second objective. The enemy's answering artillery fire was considerable from about half an hour after zero till midday, then it died away altogether. Our attack was completely successful, and after the repulse of the counter attack at NIERGNIES very little opposition was encountered. Colonel Walker went to the HQ of the attacking infantry brigades (11th and 72nd) at NT SUR L'EUVRE and stayed there during today. Major Rourke, 2i/c, left over last night and took over command of the brigade, and established the Bde HQs on the hill S of MT SUR L'EUVRE soon after zero hour.	Sheet 57B

Army. Wt. W1285g/M1297. 750,000. 1/17. D, D & L, Ltd. Forms/C2118/44.

Place	Date	Hour	Summary of Events and Information	Remarks and references to Appendices
In the Field	Oct 9		During the early morning the Infantry found on EAWNET (and Sheet 57E marking with very little resistance, penetrated to the Eastern edge of CROISILLES. The method of advance is now adopted [an advanced guard consists] Shell consists of one brigade of Infantry, one brigade of Field Artillery, one section of 60-pdrs., and a detachment of RES. The next S/th artillery is grouped in depth, in support, and will only be called upon if serious opposition is encountered. The k/Bdes. of Field Artillery will form the advanced guard like in turn. The 178 Bde is for the time in support, and will follow up at an average distance of 6000 yards from the line held by the Infantry. During today the Infantry and batteries remained in the same places as yesterday. During the morning the 87th Fd. moved up into the area between CAMBRAI – LE CATEAU had . The Infantry have advanced as far as the Eastern edge of RIEUX and AVESNES – ST. AUBERT. AWONET	

WAR DIARY / INTELLIGENCE SUMMARY

Army Form C. 2118.

Place	Date	Hour	Summary of Events and Information	Remarks and references to Appendices
In the hills	Oct 11		During the morning the Bde. moved up to the PONT DES VAQUES on the CAMBRAI–SOLESMES road and the batteries came into action in valleys to a mile & more further west. Sheet 57E

They were shelled fairly heavily, these positions, and a good number of horses were killed in the wagon lines.

The infantry we were meeting with strong opposition in ST AUBERT. The Rifle Brigade attacked the village in the afternoon but were driven back with heavy losses. The resistance offered by the enemy is not such as to suggest that he is trying to hold any particular line. His object seems to be simply to hold us up at any suitable place which offers itself to defend, causing us as many casualties as possible, then to retreat skillfully, keeping causing as he goes back with him. If this is his object, he is succeeding in attaining it. | Sheet 57E |

WAR DIARY
or
INTELLIGENCE SUMMARY

Army Form C. 2118.

Place	Date	Hour	Summary of Events and Information	Remarks and references to Appendices
In the field			The enemy having evacuated ST. AUBERT during the night, our infantry followed him and engaged him in the high ground 3000 yards East of the village. Bde. HQrs. moved up into ST. AUBERT and the Batteries came into action on the Eastern edge of the village (V.13). At 6pm the patrol on HAUSSY, 3/6 Bn. and 2 Bde. R.F.A., made by our troops in the village, and returned to the neighbourhood of COURIR for the night.	Sheet 57A
	-13			
	-14		The Bde. was relieved by the 206 Bde. R.F.A., and returned to the neighbourhood of COURIR for the night.	Sheet 57B
			HQrs. came back to the quarry at MT. SUR L'OEUVRE, and the Batteries to some open ground between PROVILLE and the FAUBOURG DE PARIS, and the Bde. rested.	
	-15		The Bde. rested for the day in this area.	
	-16		The Bde. marched to LAGNICOURT and were billetted in the outskirts. Sheet 57B	
			The Bde. entrained at BAPAUME, destination STEENWERK (Sheet) STEENBECQUE detrainment: A, B, C, D Btys., HQs. (Sheet 36A). Order for entrainment: A, B, C, D Btys., HQs.	

Army Form C. 2118.

WAR DIARY
or
INTELLIGENCE SUMMARY.
(Erase heading not required.)

Place	Date	Hour	Summary of Events and Information	Remarks and references to Appendices
In the Field	Oct 17		The scheduled time of departure for A battery was 1118 hours, but actually the train did not leave till three hours later. The succeeding trains (one for each battery) left at three hours intervals.	
	-18		On arrival at STEENBECQUE the batteries received orders to march to DOULIEU. Here they were billeted for the night.	Sheet 36a
	-19		The Bde. marched forward to ARMENTIERES, and found billets in the neighbourhood of the RUE MARLE (H12). Bde. Hd. established themselves further inside the town.	Sheet 36
	-20		The Bde. remained in these positions, and the day was spent in cleaning harness, vehicles etc. Bates were started for the men at ERQUINGHEM. Nothing to report.	
	-21		The Bde. moved forward to WAMBRECHIES, a practically undamaged village about four miles north of LILLE. We will remain in rest here till further orders. The day was occupied by batteries in the cleaning of vehicles, harness etc.	
	-22			

WAR DIARY
or
INTELLIGENCE SUMMARY

Place	Date	Hour	Summary of Events and Information	Remarks and references to Appendices
In the Field	Oct-23		This day was also occupied in cleaning. Several most sincere and hearty messages of congratulation have been received by Brig. Gen. Palmer on the work performed by the 62nd Divisional Artillery during the recent fighting around CAMBRAI. The commander 57th XVIII Corps and the G.O.C. R.A. iii rd Army have both expressed their gratitude for the assistance given, after under extremely dangerous and difficult circumstances, referred to the fighting by the Brigades as a "tour de force" to the Third Army.	
	-24			
	-25		Nothing to report.	
	-26			
	-27		Church parade was held at half past two, in a hall fitted up by the gunners for a cinematograph.	
	-28		Nothing to report.	
	-29		Lieut Colonel Bulkeley, HQrs 62 D.A, allowed a lecture in the afternoon on the subject "War Savings". It was listened to and attended by officers and [?]	

WAR DIARY
or
INTELLIGENCE SUMMARY.
(Erase heading not required)

Army Form C. 2118.

Place	Date	Hour	Summary of Events and Information	Remarks and references to Appendices
[illegible]	Oct 30		Sports were held on a German aerodrome near the village during the afternoon. Major R.F.W. Pascoe DSO, RTA, has joined the Bde. and assumed command of B battery. D battery went forward to WATT R=LOS, there Shet37 to remain in reserve under the orders of the Bt Bde RTA.	
	31		The Sports were concluded. The accoutrement of the Divisional Band Dress Uniforms were handed to apprentices. 2nd Lt 97F Steeltone D battery has been awarded the Military M.C. for services rendered with the fighting on Oct. 8.	

WAR DIARY 178th Bde RFA
or INTELLIGENCE SUMMARY

Army Form C. 2118.

Place	Date	Hour	Summary of Events and Information	Remarks and references to Appendices
Hiels	1/11/18		The Bde is located at WAMBRECHIES near LILLE in good billets & stables. Bde Commander inspected horse lines of batteries. Football competition going strong. Match between A & B Batteries. B/178 won by 3 goals to 2.	
"	2/11/18		WAMBRECHIES. Received orders to move to WATTRELOS near ROUBAIX on the 4th inst. Football matches in the afternoon and Bde Concert in the evening.	
	3/11/18	10:00	Lieut J.E. Lobell (C/178) returned from leave to England. Church parade in Cinema hall taken by Rev F.C. Churton.	
"	4/11/18		Bde moved as a complete Bde to WATTRELOS in following order 9 times. A/178 moved off at 0900 hrs. B/178 moved off at 0915 hrs. C/178 moved off at 0930 hrs. D/178 moved off at 0945 hrs. & Bde HQrs moved off at 1000 hrs. The complete Brigade was billeted and its Horses under cover by 1630 hrs.	
	5/11/18		Bde Commander inspected all Horse Lines. Major Reid M.C. & Capt Pile 2nd i/c Batteries returned from leave to England.	
"	6/11/18		WATTRELOS. Raining most of the day. 2/Lt Enriquez demobilised country round ESTAINBOURG. Lt Col R.H. Horsfield D.S.O. joined to take over Command of the Brigade.	
	7/11/18		WATTRELOS. Col Horsfield & Col Walker went round the battery horse lines	

WAR DIARY
or
INTELLIGENCE SUMMARY.

(Erase heading not required.)

178th Bde. R.F.A.

Army Form C. 2118.

Place	Date	Hour	Summary of Events and Information	Remarks and references to Appendices
Yires	7/11/18		Battery suffering very severely from influenza (about 160 cases) M.O. attending a lot of Civilians who seem to have a very virulent type & a considerable amount of deaths are occurring.	
"	8/11/18		WATTRELOS. Conference at 1100 hrs with C.R.A. at 64th Army Bde HQrs ESTAIMBOURG referens future operations especially about details of Battle 15 Corps off on 11th next position for their batteries reconnoitring by B.C.s in the Area round PECQ and route to same reconnoitred.	
"	9/11/18		WATTRELOS. Col Walker left Bde HQrs and joined HQ 1st D.A. Bde Commander Inspected Harnes etc in the afternoon. Influenza still raging through A & D Batteries. Very few cases in B & C Batteries. All Batteries ordered to dump a full Echelon as selected fatting positions & refill at A.R.P. WATTRELOS. News received the Field Marshal Foch has given the enemy 48 hrs to sign the Armistice which means by 1100 hrs to-morrow. Enemy expected to sign it. Orders received to stand fast to hold the line until further orders. Bde Commander inspected all the Horse Lines 2/Lt J.R. Greadie returned from leave to England.	
	11/11/18		WATTRELOS. Armistice signed by the Enemy to come into force at 1100 hours. Terms almost unconditional Surrender. Fighting ceased at 1100 hours. Holiday granted to all men of the brigade & football matches arranged. Bde. Commander gave an "Armistice" dinner to Battery Commanders.	

WAR DIARY or INTELLIGENCE SUMMARY

Army Form C. 2118.

178th Bde R.F.A.

Place	Date	Hour	Summary of Events and Information	Remarks and references to Appendices
H.Qtrs	11/11/18 (cont)		G.O.C. R.A. XV Corps inspected the horses of the brigade at 11.00 hrs & stated he was pleased with the general improvement of the horses of most of the Batteries.	
	12/11/18		WATTRELOS. Bde. M.O. held a parade of all the brigade & lectured on methods to be taken for prevention of venereal disease & promised the men lots of yellow ointment.	
	13/11/18		WATTRELOS. Orders received to march to WAMBRECHIES on 15th inst. Nothing else to report.	
	14/11/18		WATTRELOS. Major A.L. Wilkie M.C. left for B.C. Course in England.	
	15/11/18		WATTRELOS. Batteries marched independently to WAMBRECHIES. All were clear of ROUBAIX by 10.00 hrs & arrived in new area at 15.00 hrs. Units took up their billets without being interfered with in WAMBRECHIES. 70% of the horses under cover.	
	16/11/18		WAMBRECHIES. Units settling in to their new quarters all day. Football matches arranged for the afternoon. Capt Dick Cleland M.C. returned from leave.	
	17/11/18		WAMBRECHIES. Church parade at 10.00 hrs 17th by Rev. F.C. Lhuilton. D.tails 113rd Army Bde R.F.A attached to the brigade.	
	18/11/18		WAMBRECHIES. Major S.H. Noakes D.S.O. went on leave to England with	

Army Form C. 2118.

WAR DIARY 176th Bde. R.F.A.
or
INTELLIGENCE SUMMARY.
(Erase heading not required)

Place	Date	Hour	Summary of Events and Information	Remarks and references to Appendices
Field.	18/11/18 (cont)		A view to forming a prospective Candidates for Parliament. Bde Commander inspected Horse lines during the morning. Concert arranged for the men of the brigade by C/178 B Battery at 18.30 hrs.	
	19/11/18		WAMBRECHIES. Batteries producing Ceremonial Parade for the General before the C.R.A. to take place on 22nd inst. Bde Commander inspected billets.	
	20/11/18		WAMBRECHIES. Skirt shoot out in the Chateau used by the Men of C/178 Bde R.F.A. Skirt lasted about an hour & was then forwarded & control. Count of Inquiry on the above fire was held at once. Major C.R.M. Percival D.S.O. being present. 178 B Bde Gave a dance to the officers of 40 & 50 D.A. & the Nurses of the Military Section of Sutherland Hospital. About 150 people attended. Gave a great success.	
	21/11/18		WAMBRECHIES. Bde Commander inspected all horse lines and took office visit in the morning. A Brigade recreation Committee formed under presidency of Major F.C. Blunton for the control & running of Concerts in Brienne Hall.	
	22/11/18		WAMBRECHIES. C.R.A. 40 Divn held a ceremonial parade of the brigade on parade ground to EAST of WAMBRECHIES. Parade lasted from 10.00 hrs to 11.00 hrs. Divisional Bde Sports Committee formed to arrange men for the Corps Sports. 2 Lt Burton returned from leave.	
	23/11/18		WAMBRECHIES. Nothing to report. 3 Football Matches won & lost. & tied. The following Capt. Buchman M.C. awarded a BAR to his M.C. & Lt Blundell awarded an M.C.	

WAR DIARY or INTELLIGENCE SUMMARY

Army Form C. 2118.

178th Bde R.F.A. (5)

Place	Date	Hour	Summary of Events and Information	Remarks and references to Appendices
Givet	24/11/18		Divine Service at 10.00 hrs taken by Rev. F.C. Chevalier. Special Thanksgiving Service held at Roman Catholic Church WAMBRECHIES. Final of the inter Sub-Section football competition played between B of 178 & A & E Sub of B/178 & B/178 R.F.A.	
	25/11/18		WAMBRECHIES. Bde Commander inspected horse lines of the batteries. Sgt Dymont (M390) awarded the MILITARY MEDAL.	
	26/11/18		WAMBRECHIES. Nothing to report.	
	27/11/18		WAMBRECHIES. D.A.D.V.S. inspected Bde horses for selection of Brood Mares. Bde Cross Country run held at 10.00 hours. 9 A S competitors selected to represent Bde in Corps Cross Country competition. Special Runs were WAMBRECHIES. Nothing to Report.	
	28/11/18		WAMBRECHIES. Lecture on Demobilization held in ROUBAIX. Lorries did not turn up so men from Brigade unable to attend. Bde Commander inspected Horse Lines. Smoking Concert held in the Cinema Hall WAMBRECHIES for the officers & men of 40 & D.A. Concert opened by men	
	29/11/18		WAMBRECHIES. Gen. Vaughan, Director of Remounts GHQ inspected the horses of the Bde at 13.30 hours. Bde football & Boxing matches held during the afternoon.	

H.E. Relf Capt R.F.A.
Adj 178 Bde R.F.A.

178th Bde RFA

(1) December

WAR DIARY or INTELLIGENCE SUMMARY.
(Erase heading not required.)

Place	Date	Hour	Summary of Events and Information	Remarks and references to Appendices
	1/12/15		Church parade at 1045 hours taken by Capt F.L. Edwards. Special thanksgiving service for men of Brigade. faith at Lille at 1500 hrs.	
	2/12/15		WAMBRECHIES. Gout of Brigade inf absence of district hrs of No 2 and P. 336 D.2. M. Corby. (C/178) at 0900 hrs. Bde Commander inspected all horse lines during the morning. No. 2. Gun only Boxing Competition took place at 1400hrs in the Cinema Hall WAMBRECHIES.	
	3/12/15		WAMBRECHIES. Bde Commander inspected cooking & Washing arrangements of the units. Nothing else fresh to report. Boxing Competition in the afternoon	
	4/12/15		WAMBRECHIES. 1st finals of the No. 3 W Bty Boxing Competition took place this afternoon. The Bde won three events. Bde Commander went to Calais in H Corps Car.	
	5/12/15		WAMBRECHIES. 2nd Round HQ. DA football Competition played in the afternoon 178 I Bde DAC by 16 goals to nil. 64 F Army Bde RFA beat 181st Bde 2 goals to 1 goal. Bde Commander inspected all horse lines Bde Commander, Bde Major & Adj dined	
	6/12/15		in LILLE WAMBRECHIES. Photograph taken of the officers of the 178 F. Bde & also this members of the HQ. DA Staff. Nothing else to report. 178 F Bde concert keep goes a concert from 1830 hrs to 2030 hrs in Cinema Hall to the officers & men of HQ DA	
	7/12/15		WAMBRECHIES. H.M. the King visited ROUBAIX & LILLE. Levels of division Boxing competition took place at TURCOING. 178th Bde got line 2 prizes	
	8/12/15		WAMBRECHIES. Church parade at 1000hrs. HQ D4. Cross country run took place at 1430 hrs from Bllt & Mess.	

WAR DIARY
178th Bde R.F.A.
INTELLIGENCE SUMMARY

December 1918 — Army Form C. 2118.

Place	Date	Hour	Summary of Events and Information	Remarks and references to Appendices
Brias	9/12/18	M	Final round of HQ & D.A. football competition took place at 2 pm. Cup to L/Bty D.A.C.	
	10/12/18	T	Ground at WAMBRECHIES. 178th Bde RFA. X 64th Army Bde RFA. Harriers over 178th Bde line by Sports Officer MLB.	
			Old Cinema opened in WAMBRECHIES S. Hall. Ben Commodus inspected the Horses of A & B Batteries. Demobilisation of Miners commenced.	
	11/12/18	W	Capt Morris 9 R.F. B. St. John Steere joined & were posted IF F/178th R.F. (Yeops) D.L. Hreloch attempted his acting rank. 2nd Lt Emmett posted to B/178th. Bde RFA. 16 Miners demobilised.	
	12/12/18	T	WAMBRECHIES. Lectures on FLYING by Capt. C.R. ALSTON R.A.F. at 1430 hrs. Broken lorry closed all Blanked of Bde. Bde Concert troupe gave performance 18.30 hrs. 2nd Lt Shurt appointed Demobilisation Officer & Games Demobilised.	
	13/12/18	F	WAMBRECHIES. Bde received orders to march to WATTRELOS for demobilization by G.O.C. H.Q. Bri'd Lt. Gen. Morgan. Bde left here at 1100 hours & arrived at WATTRELOS at 1530 hrs. Are Billetted in old Mills. 178th F Bde were to play against 119th th Inf Bde on 18 in next for semi-final of Division football competition.	
	14/12/18	S	WATTRELOS. Owing to near the G.O.C's ground was considered too soft/storm to [illegible]	

WAR DIARY

INTELLIGENCE SUMMARY

178th Bde RFA

Army Form C. 2118.

(3) December 1917

Place	Date	Hour	Summary of Events and Information	Remarks and references to Appendices
Suez	14/12/17 (cont)		orders received for brigade to hand back to WAM.B.P.&E. CHIEFS. Wood stout the Bde Coys Camp Equip. had won the divisional men yesterday & of tripods & will now represent the Division in the Corps men. Boards of Survey appointed to survey all Equipment of the units. Court of Enquiry into absence of 3 drivers of A/177th Bde RFA called for West Wed.	
"	15/12/17		Church parade at 10.00 hrs. Final of inter-sub-section football competition held at 1.00 hrs between two sub. sections of B/177 Bde. 'C' Sub. beat 'A' sub.	
"	16/12/17		Demobilisation of unstaff increased to suffice to other ranks the conflict with innumerable full forms arriving. Bde Commanders inspects all horse lines	
"	17/12/17		Lt Lt L Enoades (9Div) posted to A/177th Bde owing to shortage of officers in latter battery. Bde Commander instructed officers & drill of B/177 R Bty.	
"	18/12/17		Court of Enquiry held at Hd of B/177 Bde RFA into the absence to shops Lucy & Dr K. Vey. & J. Upper & J. Lockwood of A/177th Bde RFA. Semi-final of the football competition played at CROIX 178th Bde RFA running out to match in one against 13th Div. Royal Inniskilling Fusiliers.	

WAR DIARY or INTELLIGENCE SUMMARY

Army Form C. 2118.
178th Bde R.F.A. (A)   Dec. 1918.

Place	Date	Hour	Summary of Events and Information	Remarks and references to Appendices
Field	19/12/18.		Lecture by 2/Lt Stokes Ashhurst on "Reconstruction of Civil Life" given in the Cinema Hall WAMBRECHIES at 1800 hrs. Bde Commander went round all billets &c.	
"	20/12/18.		3rd Army Band performed in the Cinema Hall WAMBRECHIES at 1800 hrs. Bachelor performance. D.A.D.V.S. inspected all horselines & pronounced 12 horses.	
"	21/12/18		Capt Harris (A/178) went on leave.	
"	22/12/18.		Church Parade at 1000 hrs in Cinema Hall. 60 Reinforcements arrived without rations having been marched all round the country & in very mutinous condition. Both allotted to the Brigade. Major Atkinson M.C. returned from leave in Bde and commanding 19th Dec 1918. Lt Gabell arrived A/178 Bde Strength on being Reinforcements from hospitals & to Bde land.	
"	23/12/18		Stores for Xmas did not arrive until 22.00 hrs. Distribution to units very awkward & very late.	
"	24/12/18		Xmas day. Xmas Church Parade at 1000 hrs in Cinema hall.	

Dec 1918
Army Form C. 2118.

WAR DIARY
172ⁿᵈ Bde R.F.A.
INTELLIGENCE SUMMARY

(Erase heading not required.)

Place	Date	Hour	Summary of Events and Information	Remarks and references to Appendices
Field	25/12/18		NAMBROCHIES. All Batteries gave their men a splendid dinner & the Bde Commander made a very excellent speech to each unit, wishing amongst the troops excellent at present. God knows what weather.	
"	26/12/18		8th C. Harrow. Capt Buchman M.C. attached to A/172ⁿᵈ during absence of Capt Morrison on leave.	
"	27/12/18		All Officers of the Bde came to Bde HQrs to see a Cinema Confidential reports.	
"	28/12/18		G.O.C. R.A. postponed his parade owing to very bad weather. Run issued. Bde Commander inspects horse lines in the afternoon.	
"	29/12/18		Bde Church Parade — Padre McLean	
"	30/12/18		Bde Commander instructed A & D Batteries to arrange Prize & Whist Drive. Divisional football competition between 172ⁿᵈ Bde RFA to represent 10th Div. K.O.S.B. 2 goals. Thus this brigade gets 2nd in the competition if our men find quality.	
"	31/12/18		Nothing to report, raining all day.	

N B Pell Capt RFA
31/12/18

178 F Bde R.F.A.
Francorp (1)
Army Form C. 2118.

WAR DIARY
or
INTELLIGENCE SUMMARY.
(Erase heading not required.)

Place	Date	Hour	Summary of Events and Information	Remarks and references to Appendices
Francorp	1/1/19		All horses of "A" "B" Battries sent Centrale into stables for a.b.c. & D. by D.A.D.V.S. 40 Div. Lt Gathrey demolished gantry	
"	2/1/19		G.O.C. 40 Div. held General Inspection of all units in Brigade drill seeing Drill, Gun Drill Stables etc and expressed himself as being very pleased with the turn out of the men & horses. B.de Commander inspected C & D Battery Stables	
"	3/1/19		All horses of C & D Battries sent to wit respective stores at 8 C & D by D.A.D.V.S. H.Q. D Sub Count of Bigomy held at Hopre into the loss of two horses of 178...	
			Capt. Stock Rhodes M.C. (proceed) Lt. Lait of 25 Brintes (murdering)	
"	4/1/19		Horses of Hopre A/178 = B/178 & Battries classified by D.D.V.K corps for demobilision. Lt. Shirlow R.F.A. took over Highland during absence of the officer on special leave	
"	5/1/19		Court of Enqy held at B/178 officer over by Capt G. No Buchman M.C. (pres) Lt. Payn & Lt. McCreadie into the loss of 2 horses by B/178	
"	6/1/19		Lecture on "Leagu of nations" by Rev Knox Recumber at Cinema Provinghus at 5.30 p.m.	

Army Form C. 2118.

WAR DIARY
or
INTELLIGENCE SUMMARY.

178 Bde R.F.A.

January 1919. (2)

(Erase heading not required.)

Place	Date	Hour	Summary of Events and Information	Remarks and references to Appendices
Field	7.1.19	Nil		
	8.1.19		East Battery played their 2nd match in the Divisional football league. Original arrangements informed D.A. he could not work 9½ hours in demobilisation	
	9.1.19		Lecture on "Democracy" at Cinque Theatre by Capt Gough; attended by 2 offrs & 30 O.R.; also D.A. Event troop held carnival in cinema Hall Doulaberies.	
	10.1.19	Nil		
	11.1.19		East battery played their 3rd match in 90 D.A. football league. Event of Gunnery held in a horse lost by A/178.	
	12.1.19		Lt. H. H. Boyce C/178 demobilised	
	13.1.19		Adjutant returned from leave in U.K. & Lt Stockson returned to B/178.	
	14.1.19		2/Lt Rocholme M.C. Driver H. Smith Lt Lt. D.H. Sports B/178 have been forwarded to England.	
	15.1.19		Demarcating Rods for H.Q. Lt D.H. Sports B/178 from the Hq. of 89 & 178 Bdy R.F.A.	

Army Form C. 2118.

178th Bde R.F.A.
Jan 1919
(3)

WAR DIARY
or
INTELLIGENCE SUMMARY.
(Erase heading not required.)

Place	Date	Hour	Summary of Events and Information	Remarks and references to Appendices
Gieed	15/1/19		State guards mounted 9 Bde today. Officers received to visit all Officers during morning to prevent stealing of horses by the French. Football health during afternoon.	
	16/1/19		Court Martial held at 6° Lethurs. 2/Lieuts Dr. Roberts + Lt. Sis Lee at 60th Bde. Major SH Noakes was President.	
	17/1/19		1st Day of 40th B.D.t Sports. Bdes did very well running most of the heats in events when not had entries.	
	18/1/19		2nd & Finishing day modified ? 2nd day of 40th D.t Sports, the Bde won a considerable amount of events.	
	19/1/19		6 Lieut Brush in the Morning & football matches in the afternoon.	
	20/1/19		Lieut Morris attached to the A.S.C & the Agriculturist party was relieved to units. Lecture by Mr L Barker on CZECHO SLOVAKS ?	
			Such & Ilayes at 5pm in Covent Hall. Horses not already sound is 9644 & Army Bdes for slaughter. All Horses of the Bde being trained.	
	21/1/19		Court of Enquiry held into the absence of 93rd C. GAUNt P (HUSAR) at 3/172 Bde (men Corpl Sich - Lieut Macleod was President LG. A Staughton LL. Burton was Australia yesterday.	

178th Bde R.F.A.
Jan 1919.
(4)

WAR DIARY
or
INTELLIGENCE SUMMARY.

Army Form C. 2118.

Place	Date	Hour	Summary of Events and Information	Remarks and references to Appendices
France	21/1/19		63 Men of 178th Bde R.F.A. marked "C2" and declared unfit Li N SERRES staying Complete demobilisation. 2 hours from these sent as drafts to "B" Batt: Brigade Battery R.F.A. with complete Harness & Equipment Etc.	
"	22/1/19		Artillery point moved to LE BREUC.R. Sheet 36. L. 15.a. 86. 2nd Lt. Wilkinson demobilised.	
"	23/1/19		Nothing to report	
"	24/1/19		Lt McDonald went on leave.	
"	25/1/19		2nd Lt McCredie was demobilised. Football match between teams composed of B & C. Battery Xmas teams composed of A & D Batteries to pick a Brigade team.	
"	26/1/19		Church Parade. Very heavy frost.	
"	27/1/19		2nd Lt Land was demobilised. Very heavy frost.	
"	28/1/19		Nothing to report.	
"	29/1/19		"	
"	30/1/19		"	
"	31/1/19		2nd Lt Fairburn with party went to 5th Army Slaying Camp. PETIT ROCHIN.	

Walter B Pets Capt R.F.A.
adj 178th Bde R.F.A.
31/1/19.

178 Bde. R.F.A.

Vol 33

Army Form C. 2118.

WAR DIARY
or
INTELLIGENCE SUMMARY.
(Erase heading not required.)

Place	Date	Hour	Summary of Events and Information	Remarks and references to Appendices
Marquette	1/2/19		NIL	
	2.2.19		Church Parade in morning.	
	3.2.19		NIL	
	4.2.19		Officers Conference at 7 Grenade Res. Rouleaux. B/W. Sample on "Reports Reconstruction"	
	5/2.19		NIL	
	6.2.19		Lecture at Roubaix by Lieut of Edinburgh. B8m. Gun. 8/178 Capt R.B. "118 Bn RFA	
	7.2.19		Lecture at Roubaix by Mr Hilaire Bellis. 2 Lieut S.E. Jones proceeded	
	8.2.19		on leave	
	9.2.19		Major A.L. Mickie M.C. 20/178 proceeded on leave	
	10.2.19		NIL	
	11.2.19		Lecture on "BOLSHEVISM" by Mr Miller at Queens Hall WAMBRECHIES.	
	12.2.19		5/R Army Boxing Competition commenced at Lille.	
	13.2.19		18" 2nd animals sent to LINSELLES Horse Shipping Camp	
	14.2.19		NIL	
	15.2.19		Capt M.D. Pile Adjt 178 Bde RFA to U.K. for demobilisation Lieut Nicholson	

WAR DIARY
or
INTELLIGENCE SUMMARY.

Army Form C. 2118.

Place	Date	Hour	Summary of Events and Information	Remarks and references to Appendices
Mosquith	15.2.19		Capt'd Adjutant (actg) XV Corps No QE 13/70. dl 22.2.19	
	16.2.19		Lieut G. McL. BROWN. M.C. posted to B/178 from X/40 T.M.Bty. Church Service	
	17.2.19		Court of Enquiry held at 13/78 Msor by Major K.C. Atkinson. Lieut St. MacDonald & Lieut McL. Brown. ref. bicycle stolen from B/178	
	18.2.19		Ord. Shoes	
	19.2.19		Nil	
	19.2.19		Capt. H. Weeks proceeded on leave.	
	20.2.19		Nil	
	21.2.19		2/Lt P. Wood C/178 proceeded on Draft Conducting duty	
	22.2.19		50 Animals sent to Kinsella Camp	
	23.2.19		Church Service. 10 Animals to Kinsella	
	24.2.19		Nil	
	25.2.19		Court of Enquiry held at A/178 Msor by Major Stn. Noakes 2920 (Pte) Capt J.A. hotrie & Edwardlhes ref. 2 horses stolen from A/178 stables Balce allotted to the Brigade	
	26/2/19		Rae. lost to 8" H.G.C. 3-1 in 2nd Round Army Cup	

Army Form C. 2118.

WAR DIARY
or
INTELLIGENCE SUMMARY.
(Erase heading not required.)

Instructions regarding War Diaries and Intelligence Summaries are contained in F. S. Regs., Part II. and the Staff Manual respectively. Title pages will be prepared in manuscript.

Place	Date	Hour	Summary of Events and Information	Remarks and references to Appendices
Macquette	27.2.19		"X" & "Y" Coys inspected by Remount Branch 50 Coy Fifth Army. Cross Country Run. Bell Huan placed fourth. Cadre "A" adopted.	
	28.2.19		Farewell Concert by Miss Ena Ashwell's Party.	

J.S. Brothers
Capt & OC

178 Bde RFA

Vol. 34

WAR DIARY
or
INTELLIGENCE SUMMARY.
(Erase heading not required.)

Army Form C. 2118.

Instructions regarding War Diaries and Intelligence Summaries are contained in F.S. Regs., Part II. and the Staff Manual respectively. Title pages will be prepared in manuscript.

Place	Date	Hour	Summary of Events and Information	Remarks and references to Appendices
Wambrechies	1/3/19		Code "A" adopted for all Batteries.	
	2/3/19		Church Parade at Wambrechies Cinema 10.00 hours.	
	3/3/19		—	
	4/3/19		All remaining "Z" animals sent to LINSELLES Staging Camp.	
	5/3/19		Conference at D.A.D.O.S. Office, Rue de Lille, ROUBAIX at 10.30 hours. Attended by an officer from each Bty. Subject — UNIT EQUIPMENT.	
	6/3/19		All ranks warned to keep sharp look-out for store thieves. Many hitems now being stolen.	
	7/3/19			
	8/3/19		2 "Y" animals C/178 sent to TURCOING Camp.	
	9/3/19		Church Parade at Wambrechies Cinema 10.00 a.m.	
	10/3/19		"X" animals sent to TURCOING Camp B/178 4. C/178 4. D/178 2	
	11/3/19			
	12/3/19		Lieut Col R.M. Hatfield D.S.O. posted to command 245th Bde RFA.	
	13/3/19		"X" & D. Horses sent to LINSELLES Camp. HQ/178. 2. B/178. 4. C/178. 10. D/178. 4.	

WAR DIARY
or
INTELLIGENCE SUMMARY.
(Erase heading not required.)

Army Form C. 2118.

174 Burma

Place	Date	Hour	Summary of Events and Information	Remarks and references to Appendices
Wambrechies	13.3.19		Court of Enquiry into absence of 99448 Pt. T. McVay a/17B. President Capt Gr. Buchanan M.C. B/178. Lieut H.Whittles B/178 & 2/Lt. S.S. Jones a/178 members.	
	14.3.19			
	15.3.19		man declared a deserter.	
	16.3.19		Church Parade at Wambrechies Cinema Hall at 10.00 hours.	
	17.3.19			
	18.3.19		41 Animals sent to Rivelle Ageing Camp. a/178 E. B/178 8. C/178 23. a/178 2	
	19.3.19		One man par. Bty posted to 40" Div. Amm. Column. 19 animals sent to Rivelle Ageing Camp. a/178 6. B/178 8. C/178 5.	
	20.3.19		911. M.E. Dyer, R.A.S.C. detected no check animal accounts of this Brigade. 2 officers & 17 men posted to Army to Organization. Attempt made by horse thieves to raid a/178 horse lines during night. 30 animals sent	
	21.3.19		Effort frustrated by alertness of piquet. a/178 2. a/178 10. B/178 12. to Tourcoing. H.Q/178 6.	

Army Form C. 2118.

WAR DIARY
or
INTELLIGENCE SUMMARY.
(Erase heading not required.)

Instructions regarding War Diaries and Intelligence Summaries are contained in F. S. Regs., Part II. and the Staff Manual respectively. Title pages will be prepared in manuscript.

Place	Date	Hour	Summary of Events and Information	Remarks and references to Appendices
Wambrechies	21.3.19		36 Arrivals sent to Linselles Camp. HQ. 4. A/178. 1. B/178. 4. C/178. 14. D/178. 13. 32 mules received from 40" D.A.C. 8 per battery.	
	22.3.19			
	23.3.19		Church Parade at Wambrechies Cinema Hall at 10.00hrs.	
	24.3.19		Commencement of new Football League designated Inter Cadre League. Drawing day for Rote. A/178. 0. 139"F.A. 7. B/178. 2. 136"F.A. 3. C/178. 0. 135"F.A. 2. D/178. 0. 23rd Canc. Field.	
	25.3.19			
	26.3.19		Football matches played 137 Field Amb 1. B/178. 1. 136"F.A. 1. C/178. 2. 135"F.A. 3. D/178. 0.	
	27.3.19		Major C.R.W. Brewer R.A.O. B/178. to England. W.O. Tel. 674. A.G.6. S.B.19.	
	28.3.19		Batts for Brigade Football League cancelled, fresh arrangements being made.	
	29.3.19			
	30.3.19		Church Parade at Wambrechies Cinema Hall at 10.00hrs. 18 Arrivals	

Army Form C. 2118.

WAR DIARY
or
INTELLIGENCE SUMMARY.
(*Erase heading not required.*)

Instructions regarding War Diaries and Intelligence Summaries are contained in F. S. Regs., Part II. and the Staff Manual respectively. Title pages will be prepared in manuscript.

Place	Date	Hour	Summary of Events and Information	Remarks and references to Appendices
Wimereux	26.3.19		sent to Rouelles Camp. 2 +13/178. 2 each. 6 +27/178. 4 each.	
	21.3.19			

J. Weeks
Major T.F.A.
COMMANDING 79th BRIGADE R.F.A.